Discovering Librarians:

Profiles of a Profession

Edited by
Mary Jane Scherdin

Association of College and Research Libraries
American Library Association

Association Of College & Research Libraries
A Division of the American Library Association

Published by the Association of College and Research Libraries
A Division of the American Library Association
50 East Huron Street
Chicago, IL 60611

ISBN 0-8389-7753-7

Printed on recycled paper.

Printed in the United States of America.

Contents

Section III: Additional Information about Librarians and the MBTI®

Section IV: Looking Ahead

Acknowledgements

My deep appreciation goes to Edgewood College for supporting me in this endeavor—particularly Donna Fuelleman for her patience and attention to detail that led to a beautiful finished product. My gratitude also goes to the Edgewood College Library Staff and Academic Dean Judith Wimmer for helping to lighten my load during the writing and editing of this book. Amanda Okopski, a creative and talented student at Edgewood, contributed ideas and drawings.

Special thanks to Evonne Schaeffer, formerly of Consulting Psychologists Press (CPP), who invited me to creatively explore possibilities for this project, and to Al Hammer, Senior Scientist at CPP, for his thoughtful counsel. Margaret Myers was a patient advisor and served as ALA liaison during the entire project. The ACRL Task Force on Vocational Interest Inventories contributed ideas, while generous funding from both ACRL and the Office for Library Personnel Resources enabled this project to go forward.

My daughter, Amy Scherdin, and my friends, Sandy Pfahler, Theresa Duello, and Bill Wera, critiqued, helped make decisions, came up with the right words when I needed them, and encouraged me to perservere. A word of thanks to Barbara Pilak who brought her enthusiasm, energy, and organizational skills to the mailings required for this project.

My mentor and friend, Jane Robbins, gave me the support and inspiration I needed to begin as well as finish my dissertation, thus leading to this larger project. Little did I know what was ahead of me when Anne Beaubien called me one day almost four years ago and said, "I just read your dissertation! Are you interested in doing more research in this area?"

Mary Jane Scherdin
Madison, WI
September, 1994

Biographical Sketches of Contributors

David T. Bailey is Professor, Department of Sociology, Sam Houston State University, Huntsville, Texas. His Ph.D. in sociology was earned at the University of Texas at Austin. His MBTI® type is ENTP.

Nancy Boykin Bounds is Head of Cataloging and Assistant Professor at Sam Houston State University Library, Huntsville, Texas. In addition to her MLS degree from the University of Texas at Austin, she has a master's degree in sociology. Her MBTI® type is INFJ.

Indra David is Associate Dean of the Library, Oakland University, Rochester, Michigan. For her doctoral work in education at Wayne State University, Dr. David studied personality patterns of librarians in Michigan using the Strong Interest Inventory.

David P. Campbell is Smith Richardson Senior Fellow at the Colorado Springs branch of the Center for Creative Leadership. He is the author of a series of psychological tests known as the Campbell Development Surveys which include the Campbell Interest and Skill Survey. Prior to his present position, he was Professor of Psychology and Director of the Center for Interest Measurement Research at the University of Minnesota where he co-authored the Strong Campbell Interest Inventory. His Ph.D. in psychology is from the University of Minnesota.

Sheila Ann Delacroix is the Assistant Dean for Reference and Information Services at Auburn University in Auburn, Alabama. In 1991/92, during her year as ALA Minority Fellow, Ms. Delacroix chose to work on changing the profile of librarians on the SIGI PLUS and several other career guidance tools. Her MLS is from the University of Alabama.

Deborah J. Grimes is Director of Library Services at Shelton State Community College in Tuscaloosa, Alabama. A Ph.D. in library administration, Dr. Grimes served as President of the Alabama Library Association in 1993-94.

Kathleen Gunning is the University Librarian and Coordinator of Information Resources at Susquehanna University in Selinsgrove, Pennsylvania. She has read and studied the Myers-Briggs Type Indicator extensively since 1985. Her MBTI® type is ENFJ.

Richard W. Johnson is Director of Training at the Counseling and Consultation Services and Adjunct Professor of Counseling Psychology at the University of Wisconsin-Madison. He is the author of many research articles on psychological assessment and the co-author of a recent textbook in this field, *Assessment in Counseling; A Guide to the Use of Psychological Assessment Procedures*. Dr. Johnson's Ph.D. in psychology is from the University of Minnesota.

Margaret Myers, Director, American Library Association Office for Library Personnel Resources (OLPR), is responsible for providing information on recruitment, library careers, and library education to prospective students and career counselors as well as to members of the profession. The OLPR has organized an ALA Recruitment Assembly to explore ways in which the Association can implement recruitment projects.

Dianne L. Nilsen is a Research Analyst at the Colorado Springs branch of the Center for Creative Leadership. She earned a Ph.D. in psychology from the University of Minnesota and is a co-author of the *Campbell Interest and Skill Survey*.

Jennifer John Patterson received her MLS degree from the University of Texas at Austin. Her workshops on the Myers-Briggs Type Indicator were part of her work as Manager of Continuing Education and Consulting for the Texas State Library. In 1993 Ms. Patterson joined the Austin Public Library as Organizational Development Coordinator. Her MBTI® type is ENFP.

Sandra Pfahler is Associate Director of the University of Wisconsin-Madison General Library System. Previously she served as Personnel Director for the same library system and currently teaches courses for the University of Wisconsin-Extension on library personnel issues. Her MLS is from the University of Wisconsin-Madison.

Mary Jane Scherdin, Library Director at Edgewood College in Madison, Wisconsin, was administrator and researcher for the librarian profile project sponsored by the Association for College and Research Libraries. Her Ph.D. dissertation from the University of Wisconsin-Madison centered on the vocational interests of librarians. Previously she served as Assistant Dean of the University of Wisconsin-Milwaukee School of Library and Information Science. She has studied the Myers-Briggs Type Indicator since 1978 and offers group workshops for librarians. Her MBTI® type is ENFP.

Maureen Sullivan has extensive experience as a consultant to libraries on organizational development, staff development, managing organizational change, and team building. She has used the Myers-Briggs Type Indicator in her consulting work, especially in helping groups develop into teams, as well as in her work as a trainer for the Management Skills Institutes offered by the Association of Research Libraries. Her MBTI® type is ENFP.

Preface

When I was deciding on a theme for my year as president of the Association of College and Research Libraries (ACRL), I considered several issues I knew were then on the minds of ACRL members. My own inclination was to focus on image, the important yet intangible idea people have about who librarians are and what they do. At the same time I sensed a worry among those in the field that the profession was not attracting the versatile, intelligent, and creative people our society needs as the information specialists of the future. Realizing that it would take longer than a year to change the dowdy and outdated popular image of the librarian, I decided instead to concentrate on a single aspect of the problem, recruitment to the field of library and information studies.

Since I believe that people choose careers based in large part on how they perceive various occupations, I wanted to make sure that sources describing today's library and information professionals would be accurate and persuasive. It stands to reason that if someone has a negative stereotype of librarians and misunderstands what they do, then that individual will never pursue librarianship as a career.

One of my informal missions over the past twenty years has been to try to change people's ideas about librarians. I cannot get over how surprised many people are to learn that I am a librarian but that I do not have my hair in a bun or wear "ground gripper" shoes. Casual acquaintances are curious why I need a master's degree to check out a book. I hesitate to confess that I was also once a victim of the librarian stereotype. When I was choosing a career several people suggested that I become a librarian, but I was not at all interested. Only after I had worked in a library did I discover how interesting and satisfying the field was for me. So, when I see others suffering from the same misconceptions, I want to set the record straight.

The place to start with any career decision is with the individual. Clearly, people make decisions in different ways: some base them on experience or observation, others on research, still others on conversation. It is also true that people are exposed to and influenced by a variety of environmental factors including parents and other relatives, friends, career counselors, and the media. Ultimately, individuals integrate what they know about their own talents and preferences with the information they have about specific occupations and professions.

Because one of the ways people are led to consider career possibilities is through vocational interest tests, I felt it was important to update the profiles of library and information specialists which appear in these assessments. Funding was secured for a research project to investigate the vocational interests of library and information professionals, then to compare the findings with existing librarian profiles.

The two most widely used vocational tools are the Strong Interest Inventory (SII) and The Myers-Briggs Type Indicator (MBTI®). The SII librarian profile was over fifteen years old, and the information on librarians for the MBTI® was based on a limited sample of 267 professionals gathered between 1971 and 1984. I also became aware of the System of Interactive Guidance and Information (SIGI+) and DISCOVER which are interactive computer tools to aid in the selection of a career. I went through the SIGI+ program myself and was amazed that it did not suggest librarianship among the possible careers I might want to pursue. When I queried the system to find out why, it told me that "librarians do not coordinate the work of others," even though that is a major part of my real-life job and an area I particularly enjoy. When I contacted the SIGI+ developers about my concerns, they told me that their profile had to cover all types of librarians, but they invited comments on how to improve it.

I was fortunate to find Dr. Mary Jane Scherdin, then of the University of Wisconsin, who was interested in the issue and willing to do the research to update the profile in the Strong Interest Inventory and Myers-Briggs Type Indicator. Sheila Delacroix, the ALA Minority Intern during 1991-1992, worked on revising the librarian profiles used by SIGI+ and DISCOVER. Funding for the research on Strong and MBTI® was provided by ACRL and Consulting Psychologists Press with assistance from the ALA Office for Library Personnel Resources. In addition, the American Library Association supported Ms. Delacroix while she participated in this project.

Most people are curious about the relationship between personality, interests, and satisfying careers. I hope the readers of this volume will share my enthusiasm and interest in this area of research and will find ways to use the results to help recruit excellent new talent to the profession.

Anne K. Beaubien
ACRL President, 1991-1992

Section I

Overview and Recent Studies of Vocational Inventories

Marian the Librarian—The Truth Behind the Image

Deborah J. Grimes

Introduction

In 1950, Meredith Willson wrote a musical entitled *The Music Man*, in which the lead female character is Marian Paroo, a small town librarian and music teacher. The character is a self-proclaimed spinster, who must continually resist the exhortations of everyone around her, including the mother with whom she lives, to "find a man." Marian is characterized as picky, hardworking, standoffish, bookish, and, by most accounts, pitiable. The phrase, "Marian the Librarian," was coined, along with this image, in a song in *The Music Man*. Over forty years later, the image continues to permeate public opinion and remain the stereotype of the professional librarian.

A column in *American Libraries* has illustrated the less-than-complimentary ways in which librarians continue to be viewed by other people. This column, along with articles about the image and stereotype of today's professional librarian, has sparked both concern and disdain. Some librarians angrily refute the image, while others deny that image has any effect on library service. Naegele and Stolar[1] suggest that "the importance of image lies not so much in its truth as in its consequences." There are, however, consequences to both the truth behind the image as well as to the image itself. The following discussion offers an overview, based on studies of librarians' personalities and interests, of the truth behind the image. It does not, however, address the validity of personality or interest studies. For a discussion of testing related to studies of librarians' personalities, see Newmyer[2] or the original studies cited in this chapter.

Results of Early Studies

Early stereotypes, reflected in the "Marian the Librarian" image, may have grown from perceptions of the job market that opened to women for the first time in the 1870s. Prior to that time, the "prevailing assumption" was that librarians were "grim, grouchy, eccentric, and **male**" (emphasis in original).[3] As the profession began to grow in the late 1870s, librarianship became a "suitable" occupation for single women (who were generally the **only** women to enter **any** job market). From its perception of the single, generally never-married female, society created the image of the spinster librarian, with both negative and positive characteristics. It was not until the 1930s that the image was examined through scientific studies.[4]

Two of the earliest studies of librarians' personalities or interest types were conducted in 1934 by E.K. Strong[5] and in 1948 by Alice Bryan.[6] Strong developed a vocational interest profile for female librarians, drawing a sample from the membership of the American Library Association. According to Strong's conclusions, female librarians exhibited the highest interests in the outdoors, writing, music, and physical science. Lowest interests were in teaching, religious activities, and social service. No interests in the twenty-two categories were shown to be exceptionally high or exceptionally low. Librarians were grouped in a category with artists and authors. Male librarians were not tested at this time.

Using the Guilford-Martin Inventory of Factors (GAMIN) and the Strong Vocational Interest Blank, Bryan tested approximately 2,400 librarians who held positions ranging from junior assistant to chief librarian in 60 public libraries in the United States. Of the 2,400 librarians in the sample, 92% were women, a figure that was representative of the librarian population throughout the country.

Results of the GAMIN showed that public librarians were submissive in social situations and less likely to show qualities of leadership. Bryan found these librarians to be reasonably well-adjusted; however, they exhibited less self-confidence and greater feelings of inferiority. As a group, female participants in Bryan's study scored highest on the Strong Vocational Interest Blank in the "librarian" occupational group, thus indicating that their pattern of interests was most similar to that of successful female librarians. They also scored high in the artist, author, and office-worker occupations. The response rate from male participants was only 33% on the Strong; thus results should be considered tentative. They scored highest on the scale for musicians, and their interests were also similar to those of writers, public administrators, advertising men, and printers. At the time of the study, Strong had not yet established an occupational norm for male librarians.

In *The Personality of the Librarian*, Robert Douglass[7] reported the results of studies conducted in 1947 and 1948 using a battery of tests administered to 144 male and 400 female library school students. The trends identified by Douglass were similar to Bryan's: library school students were found to be orderly, conscientious, responsible, conservative and conformist, introspective, aloof and impersonal, and lacking in vigor, ambition and imaginative thinking. They, like the participants in Bryan's study, were found to be weak in self-confidence and leadership qualities.

Douglass found a few differences between male and female library school students. Male students were found to have a strong sense of responsibility and strong theoretical interests. Test results on female students showed them to be more orderly and self-sufficient than male students and strong in social and religious values. Both male and female students were more interested in aesthetic and cultural aspects of life than in scientific-technological and political-economic ideas.

Analysis of data gathered in the late 1950s on the Ghiselli "Self-Description Inventory" further confirmed these findings. Morrison[8] tested over 700 academic librarians, including administrators, middle management librarians, and non-supervising librarians. Although each group showed high intelligence, they also showed a lack of supervisory qualities or even a desire to supervise. Overall, critical leadership and decision-making skills were found to be weak; however, female librarians in the lower supervisory ranks scored higher in decision-making than their male colleagues. Bryan had spoken of the frustration of female librarians who held middle administrative positions without much chance for advancement to the few top positions held by a disproportionate number of men. Writing in 1950, she noted that librarianship had formerly been a profession where women were welcomed and could rise to the top.[9]

Male librarians were studied in 1959 using the Strong Vocational Interest Blank. They scored highest on Writing and Teaching and lowest on Agriculture and Technical.[10] Although vocational interest studies showed varying results, in general, the image of "Marian the Librarian" was consistently borne out by personality studies of professional librarians conducted between the 1930s and the 1950s.

Studies of the 1960s and Early 1970s

By the 1960s, personality studies were in vogue, and studies of professional librarians yielded more detailed personality and interest profiles. Studies by Baillie and Rainwater[11] confirmed the findings of Bryan and Douglass. McMahon[12] tested a small sample of professional librarians in Tasmania in public, special, and university libraries. She found that male librarians in the study were sociable, sensitive, prone to worry, insecure, and somewhat over-controlled. Female librarians in the study were found to be sensitive, idealistic, socially withdrawn, and slightly depressed with feelings of inadequacy. Similar to librarians studied in the 50s, both male and female librarians in the study placed high emphasis on aesthetic values and low emphasis on economic values.

In a larger study which used results from several tests administered to 648 graduates of Canadian library schools between 1960 and 1967, Denis[13] found male academic librarians to be self-sufficient, orderly, achievement-oriented, respectful of authority, conservative, conformist, kind, unselfish, and sympathetic (although not prone to helping people). Male public librarians were found to be self-sufficient and somewhat shy. Female academic librarians who participated in the Denis study tended to be independent and highly achievement-oriented; female public librarians were shown to be self-sufficient, reliable, kind, dependable, unassuming, and more willing to follow than to lead. The beginning of a shift in personality qualities was reflected in the female academic librarians' tendencies to be nonconformist and independent.

Similar results were obtained by Sladen,[14] who administered the Cattell Sixteen Personality Factor Questionnaire to 108 librarians. (Eight participants were tested for all sixteen factors; one hundred were tested for only three factors.) Low scores dominated the results in the Outgoing and Venturesome categories, while high scores dominated results in the Self-Sufficient category, indicating a high level of introversion.

In 1967, David Campbell tested a sample of 410 female librarians, drawn from "Who's Who in Library Science", with the Strong Vocational Interest Blank.[15] Campbell found that the highest interests for female librarians were writing, public speaking, music, and law/politics, while the lowest were sports and medical services. Additional scores for female librarians came from a study by Nolting of 26 students who had graduated in library science between the years 1958 and 1965.[16] Nolting's results were very similar to Campbell. He found that female librarians scored highest in writing, music, and performing arts and lowest in sports and medical services. Thus, patterns of vocational interests on the Strong began to emerge. Writing and music were consistently high, but other interests varied.

McMahon's earlier determination that "people with certain personality traits are drawn towards librarianship as a career..." was corroborated in 1969 by Goodwin and reported in Rothstein.[17] After comparing library school students with other graduate students at the University of British Columbia, Goodwin concluded that the library school students formed a distinctive personality group. Using the Sixteen Personality Factor Questionnaire, she determined that the personality profile of the library school student included the following characteristics:

Reserved vs. outgoing
Intelligent
Easily upset vs. calm
Sober vs. happy-go-lucky
Shy vs. venturesome
Suspicious vs. trusting
Apprehensive, anxious vs. placid, self-assured
Self-sufficient vs. group-dependent
Tense vs. relaxed
Conservative vs. experimenting

The study also showed another shift in librarians' personality traits with the emergence of the following characteristics:

Expedient, rule-evading vs. conscientious and staid
Undisciplined, careless of protocol vs. controlled, socially precise
Imaginative, unconventional vs. practical, careful, proper

Studies of the 1960s and early 1970s, along with those conducted by Clayton and Magrill,[18] showed little overall change in the personality or interest profile of librarians: results of personality studies continued to reflect the image of "Marian the Librarian," even during the freer and more turbulent society of the Sixties and early Seventies. The beginning of a shift toward nonconforming, imaginative librarians, however, was also evident.

Profile Shifts in the 1970s

Studies conducted later during the 1970s began to show other slight shifts in the personality and vocational interest profiles of librarians. Schmidt,[19] for example, found 272 librarians, chiefly administrators and educators, to score low on conservatism and rigidity. These results were true especially among females and younger respondents, marking a change from earlier studies and reflecting an increase in the number of women in administration and library education.

A 1977 study of 315 males and 280 females on the Strong Campbell Interest Inventory (formerly the Strong Vocational Interest Blank) resulted in the reinforcement of librarians' placement in the Artistic category. Librarians scored exceptionally high on the writing interest scale and exceptionally low on the agriculture and athletic interest scales.[20] The Introversion/Extroversion scale, which measures a person's interest in working in either people-oriented or non-people-oriented occupations, showed librarians scoring just at the mid-point, with males slightly higher on introversion.[21]

Studies of the 1970s relating personality traits to the use of emerging information technologies showed librarians to be resistant to innovation and change.[22]. Clift's study of public librarians showed that they were sensitive to the needs of others and enjoyed being helpful. Other studies showed librarians to be liberal in thinking although conservative in lifestyle.[23] Little difference from early studies of librarians' personality characteristics is evident in the studies of Frankie and Turner.[24]

A marked difference, however, appears in studies like that conducted in 1981 by Yerkey.[25] Using the Rokeach Value Survey, Yerkey examined the values of special librarians, public librarians, library school faculty, and library school students. Yerkey found high scores in the categories of self-respect, freedom, inner harmony, and wisdom. Participants were found to place little emphasis on security, pleasure, comfort, and an exciting life. Although social recognition scores were low, sense of accomplishment scores were high. The results indicate that librarians are inner-directed, meditative, liberal individuals whose rewards and motivations come from self-fulfillment rather than extrinsic sources. In general, Yerkey's respondents tended to enjoy working with ideas and people more than working with things.

Gibbons and Fortune[26] administered the Cattell personality questionnaire mentioned above to 218 school library media specialists between 1976 and 1983. They reported that participants, in comparison to the general population, were highly reserved, tense, bright, assertive, imaginative, and self-sufficient. These students, all candidates for the master's degree in Educational Media, ranked a little above average on calm, happy-go-lucky, expedient, venturesome, suspicious, and self-disciplined. Average scores were found on self-assured and conservative. Some of these results differ from those reported by Goodwin above. (See page 6.)

Vocational interest inventories, revised during the 1970s and utilized with no changes during the 1980s, recognized some changes in librarians' profiles. For example, the code "AI" for Artistic and Investigative categories, was assigned to the library occupational group in 1982 on the basis of the Career Assessment Inventory conducted by Johansson.[27] The code was changed back to "A" in 1986 despite no additional testing.

To test the appropriateness of assigned interest categories, Scherdin[28] administered the American College Testing (ACT) Interest Inventory and a job activity questionnaire to 150 members of the American Library Association (ALA) and 150 members of the American Society of Information Science (ASIS). She found a significant change in librarians' scores on the ACT World-of-Work Map, from the Applied Arts (Written and Spoken) Job Family to the Scientific Job Cluster. ASIS participants, some of whom are more involved in computer or information science than traditional librarianship, scored significantly higher than ALA participants in the Investigative category. See the following chapter for further information.

Using the Strong Interest Inventory, an updated version of the Strong Campbell Interest Inventory, David[29] studied personality traits of 213 Michigan librarians and found that participants, regardless of library subspecialty, were dominant in the Artistic type. This finding confirmed 1977 studies of the Strong Campbell inventory. Analysis of David's results showed no differences between librarians working in academic libraries or in technological environments and the general population of librarians.

Emerging Patterns

Beginning with Strong's earliest studies and continuing through studies conducted in 1990, the general pattern of the librarian's personality type appears to shift. The pattern that emerges in the 1990s is of an updated female "Marian"/male "Marion" who has been, since the 1940s, consistently intelligent, introverted, self-sufficient and interested in a life of the mind and in the arts. At the same time, studies in recent years show more interest by librarians in social services and people-oriented work than in the past. These changes also show librarians to be expedient, rule-evading nonconformists.

Of great significance for the profession, the pattern of librarians' personality characteristics and interests also includes imagination, decisiveness, self-respect, and leadership qualities in sharp contrast to those found in the early studies. These qualities point out the increasing appearance of female "Marian", rather than male "Marion," in administrative and supervisory positions. While the general profile for librarians describes an individual who is reluctant to face change, taking comfort in solutions of the past, there are signs also of librarians who can characteristically apply innovation and creativity to the use of information technologies.

Finally, there is evidence in later studies of an increase among librarians in an interest in investigative and scientific activities. While the body of studies on librarians' personalities and interests supports a conclusion that librarians as a group have common characteristics that distinguish them from the general population, there is evidence in more recent studies of a diversity of interests and personality types among professional librarians. More detailed discussion of the results of current studies can be found in the chapters that follow.

REFERENCES AND NOTES

1. Kaspar Naegele and Elaine Stolar, "The Librarian of the Pacific Northwest," in *Libraries and Librarians of the Pacific Northwest* [P.N.L.A. Development Project, Vol. IV] ed. Morton Kroll (Seattle: University of Washington Press, 1960), 99.
2. Jody Newmyer, "The Image Problem of the Librarian: Femininity and Social Control," *The Journal of Library History* 11 (January 1976): 44-67.
3. Ibid, 44.
4. Ibid, 45.
5. Edward K. Strong, *Vocational Interests of Men and Women* (Stanford, CA: Stanford University Press, 1943).
6. Alice I. Bryan, *The Public Librarian* (New York: Columbia University Press, 1952).
7. Robert Douglass, "The Personality of the Librarian" (Ph.D. diss., University of Chicago, 1957).
8. Perry Morrison, *The Career of the Academic Librarian: A Study of the Social Origins, Educational Attainments, Vocational Experience and Personality Characteristics of a Group of American Academic Librarians* (Chicago: American Library Association, 1969).
9. Bryan, *Public Librarian*, 53.
10. Joseph S. Winters, "The Inventoried Interests of Male Librarians" (Ed.D. diss., New York University, 1962).
11. Gordon S. Baillie, "An Investigation of Objective Admission Variables as They Relate to Academic and Job Success in One Graduate Library Education Program" (Ph.D. diss., Washington University of St. Louis, 1961). Nancy J. Rainwater, "A Study of Personality Traits of Ninety-Four Library School Students as Shown by the Edwards Personality Preference Schedule" (master's thesis, University of Texas, 1962).
12. Anne McMahon, *The Personality of the Librarian: Prevalent Social Values and Attitudes Toward the Profession* (Adelaide: Library Board of South Australia, 1967).
13. Laurent-Germain Denis, "Academic and Public Librarians in Canada: A Study of the Factors Which Influence Graduates of Canadian Library Schools in Making Their Career Decision in Favor of Academic or Public Libraries" (Ph.D. diss., Rutgers University, 1970).
14. David Sladen, "The Personality of the Librarian: A Theoretical Analysis," *Library Association Record* 74 (1972): 118-119.
15. David P. Campbell, *Handbook for the Strong Vocational Interest Blank*, (Stanford, CA: Stanford University Press, 1971).

16. Earl Nolting, Jr., "A Study of Female Vocational Interests: Pre-College to Post-Graduation" (Ph.D. diss., University of Minnesota, 1967).
17. Marjorie Goodwin, "Correlates of Career Choice: A Comparative Study of Recruits to Health Professions and Other Professional Fields" (Vancouver, B.C., 1972) as reported in Samuel Rothstein, "Why People Really Hate Library Schools," *Library Journal* 110 (April 1, 1985): 41-48.
18. Howard Clayton, *An Investigation of Personality Characteristics Among Library School Students at One Mid-Western University* (Washington, D.C.: U.S. Department of Health, Education, and Welfare, 1968). Rose Mary Magrill, "Occupational Image and the Choice of Librarianship as a Career" (Ph.D. diss., University of Illinois at Urbana, 1969).
19. C. James Schmidt, "Librarians with the Doctorate: A Survey of Selected Attitudes and Opinions" (Ph.D. diss., Florida State University, 1975).
20. Jo-Ida C. Hansen and David P. Campbell, *Manual for the Strong Interest Inventory*, 4th. ed. (Stanford, CA: Stanford University Press, 1985), 42-43, 131.
21. Ibid, 92-93.
22. For example, Robert Clift, "The Personal and Occupational Stereotype of Public Librarians" (Ph.D. diss., University of Minnesota, 1976); Robert Presthaus, *Technological Change and Occupational Responses: A Study of Librarians* (Washington, D.C.: Office of Education, 1970), 108; and Susan S. Hamilton, "Work Motivation of Alabama Librarians: A Challenge for Change," *Alabama Librarian* 27 (January-February 1976): 4-7.
23. Sara Fine, *Resistance to Technological Innovation in Libraries* [Final Report, Parts 1 and 2] (Washington, D.C.: Office of Education, 1979).
24. Suzanne O. Frankie, "The Behavioral Styles, Work Preferences and Values of an Occupational Group; A Study of University Catalog and Reference Librarians" (Ph.D. diss., George Washington University, 1980). Robert L. Turner, Jr., "Femininity and the Librarian–Another Test," *College & Research Libraries* 41 (May 1980): 235-41.
25. Neil A. Yerkey, "Psychological Climate of Librarianship: Values of Special Librarians," *Special Libraries* 72 (July, 1981): 195-200.
26. Andrew H. Gibbons and Jon Fortune, "Library Stereotypes Studied," *Wyoming Library Roundup* 40 (Summer 1985): 33-36.
27. Charles B. Johansson, *Manual for the Career Assessment Inventory* (Minneapolis, MN: National Computer Systems, 1982).
28. Mary Jane Liskovec Scherdin, "Measuring Interests of Library and Information Professionals Using the American College Testing (ACT) Interest Inventory" (Ph.D. diss., University of Wisconsin–Madison, 1989).
29. Indra Mary David, "A Study of the Occupational Interests and Personality Types of Librarians" (Ph.D. diss., Wayne State University, 1990).

Librarians and Information Professionals: How Do We Resemble Each Other?

Mary Jane Scherdin

I. Background

Ever since the library profession began integrating computers and including information sciences in its title, questions have been raised about librarians' ability to adapt and cope. Certainly advances in technology have caused a fundamental transformation in the way information is stored and retrieved, indeed, in almost every aspect of library operations.

In the past, vocational interest inventories have indicated that librarians scored high in artistic areas and low in technical areas. (See previous chapter entitled "Marian the Librarian.") Was this truly an accurate assessment? Has the profile changed since librarians were last tested? Would persons with different types of vocational interests be needed in the future in order to meet the new technological demands? What differences, if any, divide librarians and information specialists?

To answer these questions, the author developed a study of librarians and information specialists using a vocational interest inventory published by ACT (American College Testing). Those studied in 1988 were members of the American Library Association (ALA) and American Society for Information Science (ASIS) who were asked to complete a job activity questionnaire in addition to the ACT Interest Inventory.

II. Vocational Interest Inventories

The goal of vocational interest inventories is to provide people with information that is helpful to them in identifying careers in which they will be satisfied. The inventories are based on the characteristics of job activities in a certain field as well as the interests of people currently working in that field. Edward K. Strong, Jr., who developed the Strong Vocational Interest Blank, explained that interest scores measure a complex of liked and disliked activities selected so as to differentiate members of an occupation from nonmembers.[1]

A general key to an understanding of interest measurement is found in the adage: "birds of a feather flock together."[2] The rationale is that if a person has the same interests that people in a particular job have, the person will be satisfied with that job. This is called the people-similarity or group membership rationale and is primarily empirically based. A derivative that has received greater emphasis in recent years is the activity-similarity rationale which states that if people like activities similar to those required by a job, they will like those job activities and consequently be satisfied with their occupation.[3] The ACT Interest Inventory uses a combination of the people-similarity and activity-similarity approaches.

A. Holland's Theory

The ACT Interest Inventory, is "based on the considerable theoretical and empirical work of John Holland."[4] In addition to the ACT inventory, Holland's theory is used in several widely known vocational tests, including the 1974, 1981, 1985 editions of the Strong-Campbell Interest Inventory. Holland, now an emeritus professor at Johns Hopkins University, developed four main principles.[5]

1) In our culture it has been possible to categorize people in one of six types: Realistic, Investigative, Artistic, Social, Enterprising, or Conventional. A type is a theoretical model against which people can be measured. A person's type is the product of interaction among a variety of cultural and personal forces including peers, biological heredity, parents, social class, culture, and the physical environment. First a person learns to prefer some activities as opposed to others. Later, these activities become strong interests; such interests lead to a special group of competencies. Finally a personal disposition results that leads the person to think, perceive, and act in specific ways.

2) Occupational environments can be divided into the same six types, and each will be found to be dominated by a particular type of person. Thus, the personality types of co-workers, as much as job requirements, influence the working tenor of a given occupation.

3) People search for environments that will let them exercise their skills and abilities, express their attitudes and values, and take on suitable problems and roles.

4) Behavior is determined by an interaction between personality and environment. Factors such as job performance, satisfaction, and stability are influenced by this interaction. For example, Holland points out that

Investigative, Artistic, Social and Conventional types usually do well in school because they have attitudes and values compatible with those of their teachers and thus find the atmosphere supportive.[6]

1. Holland's Models The six Holland types listed above are applied by ACT as Basic Interest Scales. Although there are lengthy descriptions of each of the six archetypal models, the short summaries used by ACT are:

> **Science (Investigative - I)** Investigating and attempting to understand, through reading, research, and discussion, phenomena in the natural sciences.
>
> **Creative Arts (Artistic - A)** Expressing oneself through activities such as painting, designing, singing, dancing, and writing; artistic appreciation of such activities (e.g., listening to music, reading literature).
>
> **Social Service (Social - S)** Helping, enlightening, or serving others through activities such as teaching and counseling, working in service-oriented organizations, engaging in social/political studies.
>
> **Business Contact (Enterprising - E)** Persuading, influencing, directing, or motivating others. Activities include sales supervision and aspects of business management..
>
> **Business Detail (Conventional - C)** Developing and/or maintaining accurate and orderly files, records, accounts, etc.; designing and/or following systematic procedures for performing business activities.
>
> **Technical (Realistic - R)** Working with tools, instruments, and mechanical or electrical equipment. Activities include designing, building, repairing machinery, and raising crops/animals.[7]

2. **Holland's Summary Scales (D/I and T/P)** The Data/Ideas (D/I) and Things/People (T/P) Summary Scales used in the ACT Interest Inventory were derived from a program of research which suggested that two bipolar dimensions underlie Holland's hexagonal arrangement.[8] (See Table 1.) The D/I and T/P dimensions also provide the basis for the ACT World-of-Work Map, as shown in Table 2.[9]

Definitions of the data, ideas, things, and people work-task categories follow. Examples are given for each category.

Data activities involve impersonal processes such as recording, verifying, transmitting, and organizing facts or data representing goods and services. Purchasing agents, accountants and air traffic controllers work mainly with data.

Table 1
Data/Ideas and Things/People Work Task Dimensions

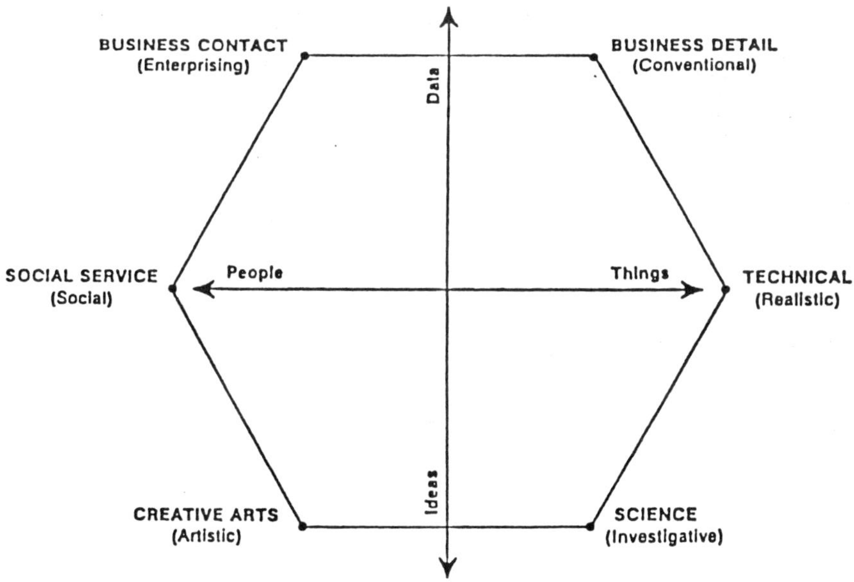

Relationship between ACT Interest scales and the data/ideas and things/people work task dimensions. (Holland types corresponding to ACT scales are shown in parentheses.)

Idea activities involve intra-personal processes such as creating, discovering, interpreting, and synthesizing abstractions or implementing applications of abstractions. Scientists, musicians, and philosophers work mainly with ideas.

Things activities involve non-personal processes such as producing, transporting, servicing, and repairing. Bricklayers, farmers, and engineers work mainly with things.

People activities involve interpersonal processes such as helping, informing, serving, persuading, entertaining, motivating, and directing others (including animals treated as if they were human). Teachers, salespersons, and nurses work mainly with people.[10]

Table 2
World-of-Work Map
(2nd Edition)

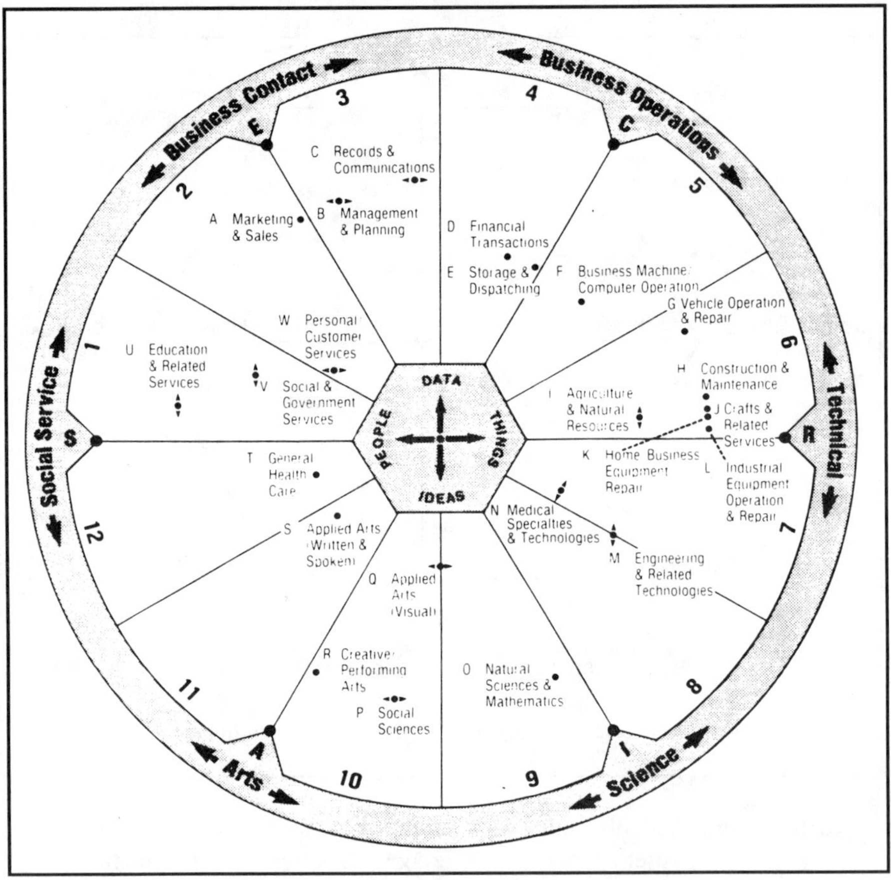

B. ACT

1. Job Families ACT grouped all 12,099 occupations found in the U.S. Department of Labor's *Dictionary of Occupational Titles*[11] into 6 job clusters (corresponding to the 6 Basic Interest Scales) and 25 job families. When occupations were grouped into job families, two components were given primary consideration: 1) involvement of D/I and T/P in work tasks as shown by the U.S. Department of Labor job analysis data, and 2) similarity of work-task-related interests as shown by occupational group scores on various interest inventories.[12] Purpose of work and the work setting were also considered. In ACT's World-of-Work Map, the 25 job families are located in 12 regions. (See Table 2.) The map is used to visually demonstrate the relationship of the job families and clusters. It is a pie whose wedges are job clusters and whose dimensions are defined by the D/I and T/P coordinates. Persons completing the test are encouraged to look into job families located in and adjacent to the map region assigned to them.

2. ACT Interest Inventory Used by one million persons annually, the ACT Interest Inventory is intended for use by individuals (junior high school students through adults) who are in the early stages of career planning or replanning. Primary purpose of the inventory is to stimulate and facilitate self/career exploration, that is, the exploration of self in relation to careers.[13]

The fourth edition of the inventory, entitled UNIACT, was used for this study. The instrument is designed to eliminate sex-role stereotyping and to be applicable to diverse populations in terms of age.

The inventory consists of 90 statements of activities, such as "learn about star formations" or "help people during emergencies," to which participants respond by choosing one of three answers:

1) I would dislike doing this activity, (0 points assigned)
2) I am indifferent, (1 point) or
3) I would like doing this activity. (2 points)

The degree to which they respond positively to six discrete sets of 15 items is the basis for giving them a score on each of the six Basic Interest Scales, e.g., Investigative, Artistic, etc. After noting the three highest scores, a three-letter code is used as a convenient summary to show the three predominant interests in ranked order, e.g. IAS. This scheme allows a simple ordering of a person's resemblance to each of the six scales, providing the possibility of 720 different patterns. In addition, a region is assigned on the ACT World-of-Work Map described above.

A second method of scoring based on the D/I and T/P work task dimensions gives a precise numerical location on the World-of-Work Map grid.[14] For each three-letter code, ACT provides D/I and T/P scores. ACT considers these scores the most accurate and has found a high correlation between them and people employed in the various fields.[15]

Overall, taking into consideration the reliability and validity evidence of the UNIACT, James Mitchell declared in *The Ninth Mental Measurements Yearbook*, "There is sufficient amount of technical evidence about UNIACT to make me believe that it is as good as its principal competitors."[16]

C. Placement on Vocational Interest Inventories
The current placement assigned to librarians on the ACT World-of-Work Map is Region 11, in the Arts Job Cluster and specifically in the Applied Arts (Written and Spoken) Job Family. Other occupations in this family are advertising copywriters, disk jockeys, legal assistants, interpreters, reporters, public relations workers, lawyers, and technical writers.

In telephone interviews conducted on December 10, 1987 and August 31, 1989, Dr. Dale J. Prediger, Senior Research Scientist for the ACT Program, stated that of the 40 occupations in Region 11, 20 were assigned to the region by the use of interest inventory scores of people employed in the field, and the other 20 were assigned by analyzing Department of Labor job descriptions. After regions were found, job families were assigned. The placement of librarians was initially based on their 1977 scores on the Strong Vocational Interest Blank and their 1982 scores on the Career Assessment Inventory. Scores for two female groups and two male groups of librarians resulted in plots which fell in Region 10 (3 groups) and Region 9 (1 group). Region 10 includes Social Sciences, Applied Arts (Visual) and Creative/Performing Arts. Region 9 is Natural Sciences and Mathematics. (See Table 2.) Based on U.S. Department of Labor job analysis information, ACT personnel placed librarians in Region 11 in the Applied Arts (Written and Spoken) Job Family.

III. Methodology
The present study examines the questions regarding placement of library and information professionals on the ACT World-of-Work Map through the administration of a job activity questionnaire and the ACT Interest Inventory. Participants were members of the American Library Association (ALA) and the American Society for Information Science (ASIS) who hold master's degrees in library and information science.

Since membership in associations does not necessarily correspond to job activities, a 17-item job activity questionnaire was devised. Its purpose was to separate activities that were classified as primarily information activities from those which were classified as primarily library activities. (See Appendix A.) The questionnaire was sent to a panel of 12 experts in the field for validation. Those questions designed to measure information activities are questions numbered 5, 6, 11, 12, 13, 14, 15, and 16. Those designed to measure library activities are questions numbered 1, 2, 3, 4, 7, 8, 9, and 10.

The random sample of 150 ALA members and 150 ASIS members was drawn from the database used for the *Directory of Library and Information Professionals*.[17] The data for this directory was collected through a questionnaire mailed in 1987 by Research Publications to update and replace *Who's Who in Library and Information Services*.[18] Drawing the sample from the Directory enabled the sample to include only those with master's degrees in library and information science. ALA and ASIS do not keep records of the educational degrees of their members.

The total number of valid responses was 198; of these 112 were ALA members and 86 were ASIS members. This was a response rate of 75% from ALA members and 57% from ASIS members.

IV. Findings

A. Job Activity Questionnaire

After calculating the responses on the Job Activity Questionnaires, it was found that there were 52 participants who spent more than 50% of their time on information science activities. This group was named the Info Group. There were 146 who spent more than 50% of their time on library science activities - the Lib. Group. Of the 86 ASIS members, 48 (56%) became part of the Lib Group, while 38 (44%) became part of the Info Group. The 112 ALA members consisted of 98 (87.5%) in the Lib Group and 14 (12.5%) in the Info Group. Thus the Info Group was made up of 14 (27%) ALA members and 38 (73%) ASIS members; the Lib Group was made up of 98 (67%) ALA members and 48 (33%) ASIS members. (See Table 3.)

After participants were divided into the Info and Lib groups, mean scores were calculated for the percentage of time spent on the two types of activities. The Info Group had means of 83.8% on information activities and 13.1% on library activities. The Lib Group had means of 80% on library activities and 10.1% on information activities. Because the mean scores of the groups were widely dissimilar, the membership of the groups appears to be clearly differentiated on the basis of job activities. Further confirmation is shown by the following data.

An analysis of the members of the Info Group showed that 29 (56%) spent 95% or more of their time on information activities, while 24 (46%) had scores of 100% on information activities. Twenty-two (22) of the 24 with information scores of 100% were ASIS members. In the Lib Group, 77 (53%) spent 85% or more of their time on library activities, while 22 (15%) had scores of 100% on library activities. Of the 22 with library scores of 100%, 21 were ALA members.

Table 3
Results of Job Activity Questionnaire

	ALA	ASIS	Total
Information Activities (Info Group)	14	38	52
Library Activities (Lib Group)	98	48	146
Total	112	86	198

Fourteen respondents were members of both ALA and ASIS; nine stated a preference for ALA and five for ASIS. Based on job activities, eight placed in the Lib group and six in the Info group.

B. ACT Interest Inventory

Percentile scores were calculated on each of the six scales of the ACT Interest Inventory for each respondent. The three highest percentiles were then used to assign a three-letter code, the D/I and T/P scores, and a region on the map, to each respondent.

The Kruskal-Wallis, a nonparametric test of statistical significance was used for analyzing all data in the study, with the .05 level being used as the measure of significance. There was no significant difference between the Info and Lib groups on the D/I and T/P scores.

The D/I and T/P scores resulted in placements in Region 9 on the World-of-Work Map for the group as a whole and all of the subgroups. The locations of the groups are approximately halfway between the circumference and the center of the circle and very close to Region 10. (See Table 4.)

Although placements of the groups in Region 9 suggest possible membership in the Science Job Cluster and in the Natural Sciences and Math Job Family, the placements are actually nearer two job families in Region 10: the Applied Arts (Visual) Family in the Arts Job Cluster and the Social Sciences Family in the

Science Job Cluster. (See Table 4 and Appendix B.) Work tasks would need to be analyzed in order to make a decision on the appropriate job family.

Table 4
World-of-Work Map
(2nd Edition)

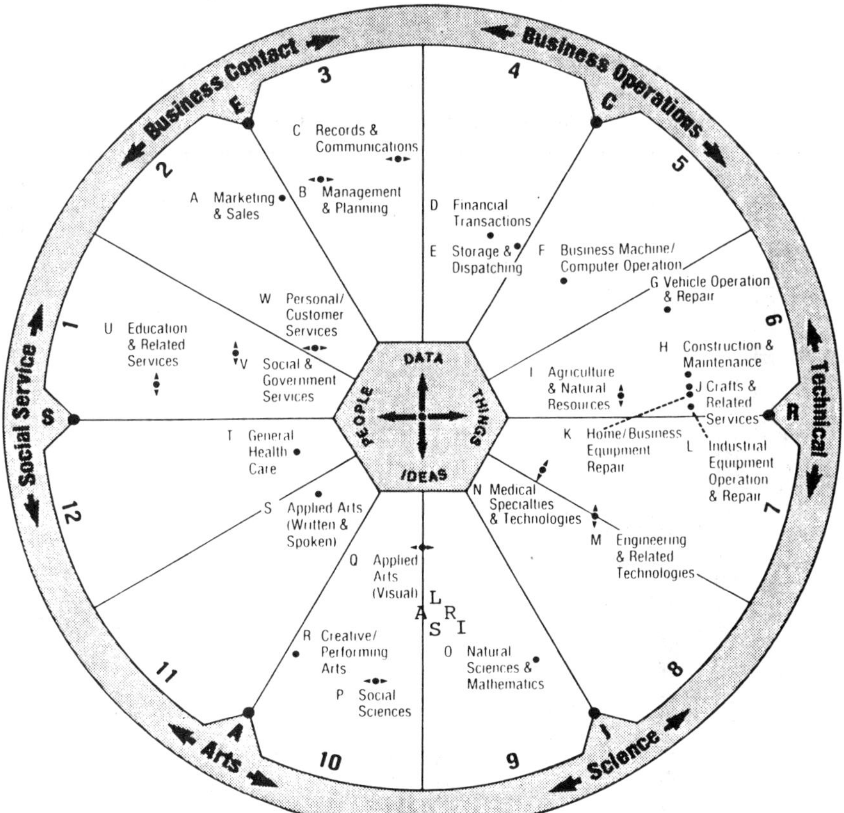

KEY

R = All Respondents, I = Info Group, L = Lib Group, S = ASIS, A = ALA

As reported above, librarians had previously been placed in Region 11 in the Arts Job Cluster and in the Applied Arts (Written and Spoken) Job Family.

Other differences between previous ACT placement and present placement are that library and information professionals show a stronger tendency to Ideas on the D/I scale and are now on the Things side of the T/P scale. The ALA subgroup placement is equidistant between Things/People, but all other groups scored slightly higher on Things. These results are similar to those found on the Strong Vocational Interest Blank in a 1977 study of librarians. On the Introversion/Extroversion scale which measures a person's interest in working with things or ideas, or in working with people, librarians fell at the mid-point.[19]

Table 5
Percentage of Groups by Region

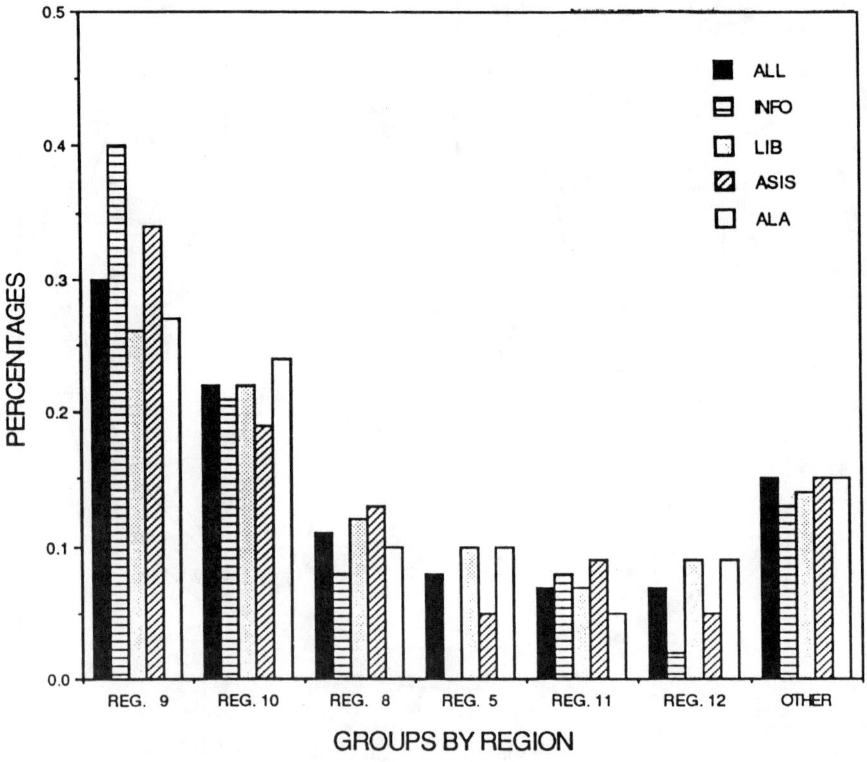

Differences were analyzed in the make-up of the groups of respondents who were placed in each of the twelve regions. Regions 9 and 10, which had the highest numbers of respondents, showed no significant difference between the Info and Lib groups nor between the ALA and ASIS members.

In addition to determining placements of the groups in regions based on the D/I and T/P scores, placements were also calculated based on three-letter codes. Results were similar to those based on D/I and T/P scores. The highest number of respondents fell in Region 9 for the group as a whole as well as each of the subgroups. See Table 5 for a presentation of placement frequencies divided by subgroup. Percentages of the groups as they placed in each region are shown in Table 6.

Table 6
Percentage of Groups by Region

	All (N=198)	Info (N=52)	Lib (N=146)	ASIS (N=86)	ALA (N=112)
Reg. 9	30%	40%	26%	34%	27%
Reg. 10	22%	21%	22%	19%	24%
Reg. 8	11%	8%	12%	13%	10%
Reg. 5	8%	0%	10%	5%	10%
Reg. 11	7%	8%	7%	9%	5%
Reg. 12	7%	2%	9%	5%	9%
Other	15%	21%	14%	15%	15%
Total	100%	100%	100%	100%	100%

Of 720 possible patterns, the most frequently found three-letter codes are listed in Table 7. (I=Investigative or Science; A=Creative Arts; S=Social Service; E=Business Contact or Enterprising; C=Business Detail or Conventional; and R=Technical or Realistic.) Only the Info Group differed in its top 3 three-letter codes. The top two are shown in Table 7. The third highest for that group was a tie between IAC and IAS at 6% each.

In addition to the similarity of the highest three-letter codes, it was shown that a high percentage of the respondents had Artistic and Investigative involved in their top three scores. (See Table 8.)

Table 7
Most Frequent Three-letter Codes

	All (*N*=198)	Info (*N*=52)	Lib (*N*=146)	ASIS (*N*=86)	ALA (*N*=112)
AIR	11%	14%	10%	11%	11%
AIS	9%	*	11%	6%	11%
ARI	7%	8%	7%	5%	9%

Table 8
Top Three Scores

	All (*N*=198)	Info (*N*=52)	Lib (*N*=146)	ASIS (*N*=86)	ALA (*N*=112)
A in top 3	81%	77%	83%	78%	84%
I in top 3	80%	90%	76%	86%	75%
R in top 3	44%	48%	43%	43%	45%

The mean percentile scores for the six scales are shown in Tables 9 and 10. The rank orders as well as the scores themselves were quite similar. One difference was that the ASIS and Info Group both had mean scores higher on the Investigative scale than on the Artistic scale, while the ALA and Lib groups scored higher on Artistic.

A significant difference was found in scores on the Investigative scale between ALA and ASIS members. There was also a significant difference in Investigative scores between the Info and Lib groups.

No significant differences were shown between ASIS and ALA members on the Artistic, Realistic, Social, Conventional and Enterprising scales. No significant differences were found between Info and Lib groups on these same five scales.

Table 9
Mean Percentile Scores on Six Scales

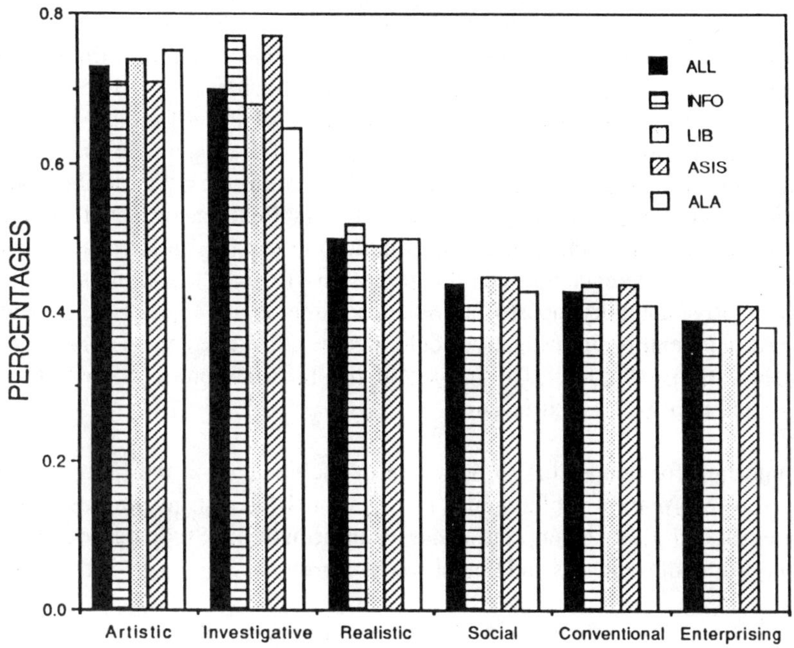

Table 10
Mean Percentile Scores on Six Scales

	All (*N*=198)	Info (*N*=52)	Lib (*N*=146)	ASIS (*N*=86)	ALA (*N*=112)
A	73%	71%	74%	71%	75%
I	70%	77%	68%	77%	65%
R	50%	52%	49%	50%	50%
S	44%	41%	45%	45%	43%
C	43%	44%	42%	44%	41%
E	39%	39%	39%	41%	38%

V. Conclusions and Implications

Librarians and other information specialists have very similar vocational interests. The one significant difference was on the Investigative scale. ACT's definition of Investigative is "investigating and attempting to understand, through reading, research and discussion, phenomena in the natural sciences."[20] Investigating through reading and research seems appropriate to a library and information professional. The emphasis on natural sciences in all 15 activity statements on this scale may have been the cause of the difference between librarians and information professionals. Examples of the statements are: Visit a science museum; Study the effects of vitamins on animals; Learn about star formations; Study plant diseases. Since the library field has attracted students from humanities and social science backgrounds in the past,[21] it is not surprising that there was a difference between the groups on this scale. It would seem that an Investigative category, apart from Science, might be an appropriate revision for the ACT inventory. Investigative could then be considered a general research and information category. The impact of the Information Age needs to be incorporated into ACT's next revision.

It is important for counselors to be aware of the changes in the placement of library and information professionals on vocational interest inventories so that they are able to give current and accurate information. Students need to be recruited from both sciences and liberal arts backgrounds.

The results of the Job Activity Questionnaire (Appendix A) showed that numerous ASIS members were spending the majority of their time performing traditional library activities, while many ALA members were performing primarily information activities. This crossover supports the conclusion that the two fields are one. Students with similar vocational interests can be recruited for the library and information profession.

If the two fields are one, library and information educators must be concerned with teaching both library science and information science courses. Computers do not need to be the central focus of one's work in order to be a successful information professional; however, coursework should be offered so that all students feel adequately prepared in the areas of technology and automation.

With the changes in the profession might come an opportunity to have its services valued more highly. Library and information workers are among the best-educated but lowest-paid professionals in the work force today.[22] If timely information is the key to today's society, then those who organize the information and make it accessible should be valued. Whether that information is found in books or computerized databases, librarians have the necessary skills in indexing, cataloging, and retrieval. The purpose is the same; the tools have changed. This study shows that librarians have shown themselves ready to meet the challenges of the Information Age. No serious differences divide librarians and information specialists.

VI. Further Research

In order to find the appropriate job family within the Science Job Cluster, an up-to-date work task analysis of library and information professionals is needed. According to Dale Prediger, Senior Research Scientist at ACT, the most recent Department of Labor job analysis was dated 1977, but the study of librarians could have been completed as early as 1970.[23]

A population not covered by this study is the group of information professionals who do not have master's degrees in library and information science. F. W. Lancaster stated that a great majority of those who call themselves information scientists and who are ASIS members have not received any formal education in library science.[24] It is uncertain what the number really is, because ASIS membership records do not include information about educational background. In addition, many information professionals belong to the Association for Computing Machinery (ACM), The Society for Information Management (SIM), or The Institute of Management Sciences (TIMS).

REFERENCES AND NOTES

1. Edward K. Strong, Jr., *Vocational Interests of Men and Women* (Stanford, CA: Stanford University Press, 1943).
2. John Darley and Theda Haagenah, *Vocational Interest Measurement* (Minneapolis, MN: University of Minnesota Press, 1955), 19.
3. Nancy Cole and Gary Hanson, "Impact of Interest Inventories on Career Choice" in Esther Diamond, ed., *Issues of Sex Bias and Sex Fairness in Career Interest Measurement* (Washington, DC: U.S. Government Printing Office, 1975), 3-17.
4. James Mitchell, Jr., ed., *The Ninth Mental Measurements Yearbook* (Lincoln, NE: University of Nebraska Press, 1985), 34.
5. John Holland, *Making Vocational Choices: A Theory of Careers* (Englewood Cliffs, NJ: Prentice-Hall, 1973) and *Making Vocational Choices: A Theory of Vocational Personalities and Work Environments* (Englewood Cliffs, NJ: Prentice-Hall, 1985), 2-4.
6. Holland, *Making,* 1985, 56.
7. *Technical Report for the Unisex Edition of the ACT Interest Inventory (UNIACT)* (Iowa City, IA: The American College Testing Program, 1981), 1.
8. Holland *Making,* 1973 and 1985.

9. Dale Prediger, "A World-of-Work Map for Career Exploration," *Vocational Guidance Quarterly* 24 (March 1976): 198-208 and Dale Prediger, "Dimensions Underlying Holland's Hexagon: Missing Link Between Interests and Occupations?" *Journal of Vocational Behavior* 21 (December 1982): 259-287.
10. *Technical Report*, 2.
11. U.S. Department of Labor, *Dictionary of Occupational Titles,* 4th ed. (Washington, D.C.: Author, 1977)
12. *Using the ACT Assessment on Campus* (Iowa City, IA: The American College Testing Program, 1986).
13. *Technical Report*, 1.
14. Ibid, 2.
15. Dale Prediger, telephone conversation with author, 31 August 1989.
16. Mitchell, *Ninth*, 35.
17. *Directory of Library and Information Professionals* (Woodbridge, CT: Research Publications, 1988).
18. *Who's Who in Library and Information Services* (Chicago: American Library Association, 1982).
19. Jo-Ida C. Hansen and David P. Campbell. *Manual for the Strong Interest Inventor* 4th ed. (Stanford, CA: Stanford University Press, 1985), 92-93.
20. *Technical Report*, 1.
21. William Moen and Kathleen Heim (Eds), *Librarians for the New Millenium* (Chicago: American Library Association, Office for Library Personnel Resources, 1988), 100.
22. Emily Fayen, "Beyond Technology: Rethinking 'Librarian'," *American Libraries* 17 (April 1986): 240-242.
23. Dale Prediger, telephone conversation with author, 26 September 1989.
24. Frederick Lancaster, "Future Librarianship: Preparing for an Unconventional Career" *Wilson Library Bulletin* 58 (May 1983): 747-753.

BUSINESS OPERATIONS JOB CLUSTER

C. **Records and Communications** Office, library, hotel, and postal clerks; receptionists; computer tape librarians; office, medical, and legal secretaries; court reporters; medical record technicians

D. **Financial Transactions** Bookkeepers; accountants; grocery check-out clerks; bank tellers; ticket agents; insurance underwriters; financial analysts

E. **Storage and Dispatching** Shipping and receiving clerks; mail carriers; truck, cab, and airline dispatchers; cargo agents; air traffic controllers

F. **Business Machine/Computer Operation** Computer console, printer, etc., operators; office machine operators; typists; word-processing equipment operators; statistical clerks

TECHNICAL JOB CLUSTER

G. **Vehicle Operation and Repair** Bus, truck, and cab drivers; auto, bus, and airplane mechanics; forklift operators; merchant marine officers; airplane pilots

H. **Construction and Maintenance** Carpenters; electricians; painters; custodians (janitors); bricklayers; sheet metal workers; bulldozer and crane operators; building inspectors

I. **Agriculture and Natural Resources** Farmers; foresters; ranchers; landscape gardeners; tree surgeons; plant nursery workers; pet shop attendants

J. **Crafts and Related Services** Cooks; meatcutters; bakers; shoe repairers; piano/organ tuners; tailors; jewelers

K. **Home/Business Equipment Repair** Repairers of TV sets, appliances, typewriters, telephones, heating systems, photocopiers, etc.

L. **Industrial Equipment Operation and Repair** Machinists; printers; sewing machine operators; welders; industrial machinery repairers; production painters, laborers and machine operators in factories, mines, etc.; firefighters

SCIENCE JOB CLUSTER

M. **Engineering and Other Applied Technologies** Engineers and engineering technicians in various fields; biological and chemical lab technicians; computer programmers; computer service technicians; drafters; surveyors; technical illustrators; food technologists

N. **Medical Specialties and Technologies** Dental hygienists; EEG and EKG technicians; opticians; prosthetics technicians; X-ray technologists; medical technologists; dentists; optometrists; pharmacists; veterinarians

O. **Natural Sciences and Mathematics** Agronomists; biologists; chemists; ecologists; geographers; geologists; horticulturists; mathematicians; physicists; soil scientists

P. **Social Sciences** Marketing research analysts; anthropologists; economists; political scientists; psychologists; sociologists

ARTS JOB CLUSTER

Q. **Applied Arts (Visual)** Floral designers; mechandise displayers; commercial artists; fashion designers; photographers; interior designers; architects; landscape architects

R. **Creative/Performing Arts** Entertainers (comedians, etc.); actors/actresses; dancers; musicians, singers; composers; writers; art, music, etc. teachers

S. **Applied Arts (Written and Spoken)** Advertising copywriters; disk jockeys; legal assistants; advertising account executives; interpreters; reporters; public relations workers; lawyers; libraries; technical writers

SOCIAL SERVICE JOB CLUSTER

T. **General Health Care** Nursing aides; orderlies; dental assistants; licensed practical nurses; physical therapy assistants; registered nurses; dieticians; occupational therapists; physicians; speech pathologists.

U. **Education and Related Services** Teacher aides; preschool teachers; athletic coaches; college teachers; guidance/career/etc., counselors; elementary and secondary school teachers; special education teachers

V. **Social and Government Services** Security guards; recreation leaders; police officers; health/safety/food/etc. Inspectors; child welfare workers; home economists; rehabilitation counselors; sanitarians; social workers

W. **Personal/Customer Services** Grocery baggers; bellhops; flight attendants (stewards, stewardesses); waitresses and waiters; cosmetologists (beauticians); barbers; butlers and maids

SIGI PLUS: A Case Study in Changing Images

Sheila Ann Delacroix

"Librarian for boarding/day school. MLS (ALA accredited), 3 yrs. experience. ***Expertise in wrestling and other sports helpful*** **" (italics mine).**[1]

It is obvious to anyone who staffs a library reference desk or catalogs the quirky products of the publishing industry, that being a librarian is a many faceted job calling for multi-talented individuals. Of course, sometimes it is hard to pin down exactly what those talents are. As the above advertisement shows, librarians are often counted on to bring unique skills to their positions, and these skills are not always the ones which the general public easily associates with librarians.

For several years I had a cartoon on the file cabinet in my office which served as a daily reminder of the diverse demands placed on the library staff. The cartoon depicted two gentlemen in an office setting. From a sign on the door you can see that this is an employment agency. The man behind the desk is saying to the person on the other side, who is obviously applying for a job, "You claim to be experienced in psychology, counseling, teaching, and arbitration. But it says here that you are just a librarian." After I taped this cartoon to my cabinet, the librarians in the reference department would appear periodically to add other areas of expertise which had come in handy that day. Some of the ones I remember were: crowd control, child rearing, medicine, mind reading, and one day after an incident the details of which have faded from my memory (thank goodness), someone wrote "witchcraft".

The questions of who we are and how we get motivated, talented people to join us in our noble profession are hotly debated and coolly considered in many arenas. However, the practical work of education and recruitment go on in spite of the theoretical debate, and we might be surprised to learn who is doing the educating and recruiting. Librarians routinely refer patrons, especially students, to sources meant to help in career selection. Perhaps, too few read what these sources say about librarians and librarianship. If they did, they might be tempted to ask, "Who writes this stuff?" In the case of SIGI PLUS, we found out.

Introduction to SIGI Plus

SIGI PLUS is a computer-assisted career guidance tool based on a theory of career guidance developed by Martin R. Katz. In his 1993 book, *Computer-Assisted Career Decision Making*, Katz says, "At this writing, the current version of SIGI PLUS is being used at more than 1,000 colleges and universities, as well as secondary schools, libraries, corporations, community-based organizations, and counseling agencies in the United States. It has also been adapted for use in Australia by the Australian Council for Educational Research."[2] Educational Testing Service (ETS), the publisher of this system, describes its product in the following manner: "The SIGI PLUS career guidance system is a comprehensive, interactive software program. SIGI PLUS (System of Interactive Guidance and Information - Plus More) is licensed by Educational Testing Service and is part of the ETS family of computerized guidance and assessment products."[3]

ETS goes on to say, "SIGI PLUS covers all the major aspects of career decision-making and planning through a carefully constructed system of nine separate but interrelated sections....SIGI PLUS's unique layering concept allows users to explore the system in different degrees of detail, depending on the amount and type of information they need. In addition, SIGI PLUS can recommend specific pathways through the system based on the user's answer to a question about his or her career status." All of this is very true. However, much of the occupational information users get from the SIGI system is based on a database of 220 "occupational descriptions" or profiles for each of the occupations treated. Like any computer system, you can only get out what you put in.

My introduction to SIGI PLUS came at the reference desk of a small university library when one of the counselors from the campus counseling center approached to ask if she could leave a brochure about SIGI with the reference staff. She said that students might come to us asking where to go to find SIGI, and the brochure would give us the information we needed to guide them. She explained that at the counseling center there was a SIGI lab which students could use. I leafed through the brochure, surmised that SIGI was a computerized career exploration tool and asked if my high school senior son, who had yet to decide on a college major, could use the system. The counselor said he was welcome to come by, so at the first opportunity, I steered my son in the direction of the counseling center. He came back several hours later with reams of printouts and said he'd had a very good time. He said the system was interesting, he had gotten some ideas, and he might go back to explore more at a later date. I didn't think about SIGI too much after that except to know that we had the brochure at the desk and to tell students where to go to find SIGI if they asked. My son went off to college a history major and by the end of the first semester turned into an astronomy major. I do not know if SIGI had anything to do with either decision.

I next encountered SIGI as I was readying an application for the American Library Association's (ALA) Minority Fellowship Program. I noticed that the Association of College and Research Libraries (ACRL), the division in which I was most interested, listed among the possible fellowship projects "working on interactive career guidance packages such as SIGI PLUS." The idea was to update the descriptions of librarians being introduced to the users of SIGI PLUS. I thought if I were awarded the fellowship, this could be a way to make a real difference during my year at ALA, by helping the profession in a far-reaching way. I decided to visit the counseling center to see just what sort of work the system might need.

Librarians and SIGI Plus

Exploring the occupation of Librarian on SIGI PLUS for the first time produced some interesting results. Under a category labeled "Description of Work Activities,"[4] I found a paragraph which read, "General librarian: orders, catalogs, organizes books, magazines, other library materials. Reference librarian: helps people locate materials and aids in research. School librarian: helps develop young people's interest in reading: teaches them to use resources. In small libraries may perform many tasks." These were the descriptions given of the THREE types of librarians. No other librarians were mentioned, not even with an "et cetera" or an "and others."

With my suspicions aroused, I returned to the beginning of the program and asked the system to compare the career of librarian with that of historian. Among other things, I came to a category labeled "Special Conditions." I found the following description for historian:

> Much work is solitary. May take many years of painstaking research, analysis, and writing to complete a major study. Discovering new sources of information depends on imagination, persistence and sometimes luck. Must read constantly, good memory essential. Years of study, analysis and reflection usually lead to increasing competence through one's working life. Finding new material or creating a fresh understanding of old material can be exciting.

At the same time, I learned that *librarians may be required to work nights and weekends, need patience to deal with the public, and may need to stoop, lift or reach to high places for books!* The effect of the juxtaposition of these answers on the computer screen was chilling.

I began going through the database looking at several different careers and comparing them to the description given for librarians. I have to admit to being comforted temporarily by some of the "special conditions" I found under other occupations. For example, the following description appeared for the occupation of anthropologist:

> Some fieldwork involves exposure to unfamiliar diseases, different diets, living in tents/huts, lack of privacy, insects, snakes, wild animals, perhaps local hostility to research project and/or general political instability. Living among people with different ideas, customs, etc. can bring a sense of isolation. Work on excavation sites is dirty, slow, often hot and tiring. Fieldwork might involve studies in urban neighborhoods. Positive factors include: opportunities for unusual, exciting experiences; enormous range of possible research topics; often great independence during fieldwork; seeing the world through the eyes of other cultures or subcultures.

Compared to the diseases, snakes and wild animals, evening and weekend hours looked pretty good. I have to say I was most uncomfortable with and disappointed in the fact that fieldwork in urban neighborhoods was listed in the negative column along with diseases, insects and snakes. (I asked myself here, as I did many times with regard to the profile of librarians, whose bias is coming through the text?) However, after listing all of the possible horrors of political instability and isolation, anthropologists could look forward to exciting experiences and seeing the world through the eyes of other cultures. On the other hand, librarians could look forward to stooping, lifting and reaching to high places for books!

Under a category labeled "Specific Occupational Training," aspiring librarians were instructed to "volunteer or do part-time work at a local library or in your college library while in school." Future historians were told about internships, assistantships, and grant-funded projects.

I was convinced at this point that librarians and librarianship could certainly benefit from a rewrite of this program. As a final test, I went into a different section of the system which asks questions and uses the responses "to create a personalized list of occupations based on values, interests, skills and level of education." I went through this section answering each question based on my actual job activities as Head of Reference Services. Needless to say, the list of possible occupations generated by these responses did not include librarian. I went through the exercise several times, making a few changes each time, leaving out one aspect of the job, including others. I could never get the system to tell me I might consider librarianship as a career. When queried as to why this career choice did not surface, the system would respond with phrases like "Librarians do not speak in front of large groups of people."

Upon receiving the Minority Fellowship and beginning work at ALA, my first step was to touch base with Anne Beaubien, then President of ACRL, who had originated the idea of rewriting the profiles. We contacted the appropriate persons at Educational Testing Service and they agreed to "consider any changes" we would like to offer. They said they were in the process of updating several profiles, librarians included, and they would love to hear from us. However, they would not love to hear from tons of people with tons of ideas. We could poll as many contributors as we wished, but in the end we were to send to ETS only one complete profile revision from the American Library Association.

Revision of Librarian Profile

To give an idea of the scope of this job, the actual profile sent to us by ETS consisted of 31 questions, two of which had ten subsections. (See Appendix A at the end of this chapter for a complete listing of the profile questions.) These questions were not able to be answered by checking off numbers on a scale, they involved looking at the profession in depth from the specific to the general. It would require time and thought to come up with answers. And just to make it really interesting, each occupation is limited in the amount of space allotted. The theory behind maintaining this approach, even though technology would allow unlimited space, is explained by Katz when he addresses the question of which occupational titles to include in the database: "A guidance system would violate the law of parsimony if it designated by separate titles two or more occupations that were identical in almost all relevant attributes."[5] For example our definition of the profession could take up no more than nine lines with 80 characters per line.

The method chosen to attack this project was based on several factors. First, I did not have the temerity to believe I was going to rewrite the profile alone. Second, I would have less than one year, and only about a quarter of my time to devote to the project, so I knew I could not cast too wide a net in search of other participants. Third, I could not depend solely on friends and acquaintances to serve as reviewers of the profile. My position at central headquarters allowed me to visit the ALA offices for the various divisions and solicit names of twenty-five librarians from a variety of types of libraries, engaged in a variety of types of activities. I looked for people who might have given this particular issue some thought from various perspectives, including education, recruitment, and public relations. I needed a broad picture of the profession and not a description of academic librarianship or school librarianship or any other specialty. Each of the lucky persons nominated was sent a very thick profile to review, comment on, and change as they saw fit. Nineteen completed responses, representing hours of hard labor by these wonderful people, were returned. Using their words, their ideas, and their experiences, I went to work building a realistic, dynamic picture of modern librarians and librarianship. Appendix B gives some examples of the original text found in the profile, followed by the text I proposed as a replacement.

The need for the suggested improvements seemed so obvious that when they were sent off to Educational Testing Service, I expected that they would be embraced with enthusiasm. Many weeks later, a packet arrived from ETS thanking me for my work on the profile, stating that they had used most of what I sent, and enclosing a copy of the new profile as it would go out in the Fall, 1992 update. Much of the text had been greatly altered to reflect my contributions. Bending, stooping and lifting had been removed. There was information about internships and graduate assistantships and post-graduate residency programs. "Intellectual curiosity" was listed as the number one personal qualification necessary to the profession instead of "love of books." Science and Mathematics were added as possible fields of interest to future librarians. Unfortunately some areas fell considerably short of being satisfactory, and a couple of areas had even been made worse through the revision process. Appendix C shows some of the changes that cried out for more revision.

These results brought home the fact that once again narrow, outdated, and biased notions of what librarians and librarianship were all about prevailed, and even testimony from the people in the profession was not enough to eradicate these misconceptions. This is very much in keeping with the ideas stated by Andrew Abbott in his book *The System of Professions: an Essay on the Divisions of Expert Labor*. Abbott posits that the public's image of a profession develops "over a period of a decade or more. Professional images do not change suddenly. ... In addition, the public seems to remember professionals in the image in which it first saw them; "Ben Casey" is still alive for many Americans. For whatever reason, public images of professions are fairly stable."[6] It should not be surprising, then, to see these results or to hear a story from a colleague who was doing research on a particular psychological profile as part of her dissertation. After she had surveyed a sample of professionals and obtained data contrary to the existing profile of librarians sanctioned by the company, she shared her findings with the person in charge of research for the company. His response was that her data might be correct for academics, but not for his little librarian at the corner branch of the public library. When assured that "little branch librarians" were also included in the sample, he was unmoved. Just as Abbott would have predicted, the data did not fit his remembrance of librarians as he had first experienced them, so the data were ignored.

I contacted ETS and registered objections to various sections of the new revision. A particularly strong plea was made for the removal of the sentence about restraining children. (See page 48.) Many missed communications and several long distance discussion sessions followed. Eventually that section was rewritten, and the revision was included in the subsequent update released in August, 1993.

Conclusion

When putting together a final report, I began to look for evidence of how others had evaluated this tool. Searching *ERIC* and *Psych-Lit* and *Dissertation Abstracts* for SIGI will yield over a hundred articles, reports and dissertations on the subject. There are entire bibliographies of SIGI related articles. But with very few exceptions, these articles report on studies of how various populations reacted to using SIGI; how different communities of users (men as opposed to women, high school students as compared to college students, disabled students versus the abled, etc.) responded to using a computer to explore their values, skills, interests and possible occupational choice. Almost nowhere in the literature is the question raised of how the occupational profiles were built.[7]

It seems obvious that a system set up to help students incorporate self-knowledge and occupational information into career decisions, needs to start with occupational information that is factually correct as well as free of subtle (and not so subtle) biases. I am also concerned that in many counseling situations, the conclusions of one dissertation writer are being played out. That writer concluded, "It is recommended that SIGI be used...because SIGI was not harmful for students and it was cost effective in terms of personnel time."[8] It is not sufficient to say, "We have done no harm," nor is it factual. It would be more truthful to say, "We have done no harm that we know about or can measure or have bothered to look for." Katz would seem to agree. He says, "Reaching many more people than any counselor, computerized systems are capable of widespread help or harm and should be held to the highest standards of accountability."[9]

Katz dedicates much of his book, *Computer-Assisted Career Decision Making,* to SIGI PLUS and its predecessor, SIGI. He spends many pages describing the research and reasoning underlying each section of these systems. The process of collecting and reviewing occupational information is summarized as follows:

> Each item of information in the system is the product of dogged applied research by dedicated occupational analysts. While sources vary from one occupation to another, they typically include professional associations, labor unions, employers, publications of many kinds (including those put out by the Department of Labor and other government agencies, occupational briefs and monographs, psychological and sociological studies of occupations, economic forecasts, and commercial surveys), and consultant panels of members of the occupation. Information gathered from these diverse sources is winnowed for each occupation, and a draft written in form suitable for the system is sent to as many as 12 selected reviewers - the number varies according to the number of specialties and environments for the occupation. The reviewers usually represent associations and unions, educators in fields preparatory for the occupation, and practitioners. Sources of information, including reviewers, are entered into a data-base management program to be consulted for updates.."[10]

There is little to fault in this chapter on how occupational information is gathered and entered into the system, except to say that at least in the case of librarians and librarianship, the procedure broke down along the way. The 1991 release of the program attributes no "satisfactions" to the profession, i.e., in a list calling for pros and cons of working in the profession, there were no pros; it ignores the fact that persons with science and computer backgrounds are needed and do find fulfillment in the profession; and it virtually dismisses the administrative and professional supervisory components of many library positions.

Three thoughts have stayed with me since the completion of this exercise in profile revision. First, there are many groups outside of librarianship, who are daily defining and interpreting our profession to others. SIGI PLUS is just one of hundreds of computerized or print career guidance tools. By raising our awareness of what is contained in these tools, questioning the producers, and volunteering to provide valid information, we can have input into how the profession of librarianship is represented to outsiders.

Second, the old programmers' creed correctly states: "Garbage in - garbage out." Yet as software packages and databases proliferate, and people turn more and more often to computers to supply all of the answers to all of the questions (with a blind faith that I find equally disturbing and easy to understand), we have to be very careful that what goes into the systems is not garbage. It is not enough to look at how much mainframe space a given database is going to need, or how much hardware must be purchased to accommodate it, or what is the best price you can get for the package. We must question the foundations of these systems. Of course, I am not just referring to career guidance systems, but also to the many packages we buy for our libraries. William Godwin writes that SIGI should be "viewed not merely as a demonstration of computer-aided education, but more as a demonstration of how technology can be used to give students more control over their lives."[11] We need to be sure that the control is being taken by the user, not by the technology.

Finally, I came away from this project with an appreciation of chaos theory as it applies to librarianship. Chaos theorists hold that the flapping of a butterfly's wings can change the climate across the globe.[12] It is obvious that there is still a need to change the climate for librarians and librarianship. By making changes in programs like SIGI PLUS, we are flapping our collective wings and changing the image now and into the future. Abbott says it takes a decade to create an image in the public's eye.[13] The next decade starts today.

REFERENCES AND NOTES

1. *Library Hotline*, 22 (February 22, 1993): 9.
2. Martin R.Katz, *Computer-Assisted Career Decision Making: The Guide in the Machine* (Hillsdale, NJ:Lawrence Erlbaum Associates, 1993), x.
3 Promotional information provided by Educational Testing Service, Princeton, NJ to potential purchasers of the SIGI PLUS system.
4. All quotations from the SIGI system are taken from the 1991 release of the SIGI PLUS software.
5. Katz, *Computer-Assisted*, 155.
6. Andrew Abbott, *The System of Professions: An Essay on the Divisions of Expert Labor* (Chicago: University of Chicago Press. 1988), 61.
7. In a 1973 speech, Martin Katz asks the question, "Where did all this information come from, and how accurate is it?" He then goes on to answer in part, "It came from more sources than I have time to list, and it is as accurate as we can make it with the help of specialists in many fields. ... However, he does end this section with a telling comment. "We did not have time," he says, "or resources to poll a large sample from each occupation on these questions....So the responses for each occupation were pooled with our readings as a basis for inference and consensus among our own staff." [Educational Testing Service, *Measurement for Self-Understanding and Personal Development: Proceedings of the 1973 Invitational Conference on Testing Problems* (Princeton, NJ: Educational Testing Service, 1974), 43-69.] As we have seen in the case of the profile for the librarian and even to some extent in the updated profile of the anthropologist, "inference and consensus" did not go very far toward filtering out biases for or against a given career or a specific aspect of a given career.
8. Charles Richard Viar, "Comparative Study of the Effectiveness of the System of Interactive Guidance and Information for Students at Dyersburg State Community College" (EdD diss., Memphis State University, 1985) abstract in *Dissertation Abstracts International* 46/11-A(1986): 3225.
9. Katz, *Computer-Assisted*, xi.
10. Ibid, 164-165.
11. William F. Godwin, "SIGI: An Operational Example of Computer Based Career Guidance" (paper presented at the National Computer Conference, Chicago, IL, May, 1974) abstract in *ERIC*, document number ED 097590.
12. There is much written on chaos theory as it applies to a variety of disciplines. One article which "explores whether chaos is an interesting idea...or a revolution in scientific thought" is Robert Pool, "Chaos Theory: How Big an Advance?" *Science* 245 (July 7, 1989): 26-28.
13. Abbott, *The System*, 61.

Appendix A
SIGI+ System
Profile of a Librarian

(1) Definition of occupation? (Give major divisions/groupings. Also give major employment areas --e.g. industry, academia, etc.) Please limit response to 9 lines of text.

(2) Description of work activities? Please limit response to 9 lines of text.

(3) Typical job titles/specialties? (Line through those that are inappropriate. Add any you see as more appropriate.) Please limit response to 9 lines of text.

(4) Work setting(s)? Indoor/outdoor? (Describe physical work settings, typical travel, and/or on-site visits, if appropriate.) Please limit response to 9 lines of text.

(5) Special problems/satisfactions? (Give the pros and cons of working in this occupation.) Please limit response to 9 lines of text.

(6) Educational requirements? Please limit response to 9 lines of text.

(7) Examples of college courses? Please limit response to 9 lines of text.

(8) Specific Occupational training? (Include traineeships, practice teaching, residencies, etc.) Please limit response to 9 lines of text.

(9) Personal qualifications? Please limit response to 9 lines of text.

(10) Most important skills? (with examples of how they are used) (All skills listed below are considered ESSENTIAL in the occupation. You may add or delete from the listing, but if you add, (a) do not exceed 10, (b) select from the taxonomy of skills that follows the listing, and (c) be sure to give SPECIFIC examples of how they are used. You may use part of a skill--e.g., just "training" instead of "training, instructing.") Please limit response to 6 lines of text following each skill.

(11) Other requirements? Expertise? (Includes certification, licensure, continuing education, etc.) Please limit response to 9 lines of text.

(12) Beginning income? (national figures) Please limit response to 9 lines of text.

(13) Median income? (national figures) Please limit response to 9 lines of text.

(14) Top earning possibilities? Please limit response to 9 lines of text.

(15) How do earnings vary? Please limit response to 9 lines of text.

(16) Contribution to society? Please limit response to 9 lines of text.

(17) Leadership? Please limit response to 9 lines of text.

(18) Prestige level? Please limit response to 9 lines of text.

(19) Leisure/flexible time? Please limit response to 9 lines of text.

(20) Independence on the job? Please limit response to 9 lines of text.

(21) Variety? Please limit response to 9 lines of text.

(22) Interest fields? Please limit response to 9 lines of text.

(23) National employment outlook? Please limit response to 9 lines of text.

(24) Where employed? Please limit response to 9 lines of text.

(25) Security? Please limit response to 9 lines of text.

(26) Advancement? (Give common paths for advancement with typical job titles.) Please limit response to 9 lines of text.

(27) Where to find out more? Please limit response to 9 lines of text.

(28) Major Work Tasks (with examples) This section is designed to give users a broad picture of how they would spend their time in this occupation. You may add new tasks; up to 12 are permitted. You may use up to twelve lines to illustrate tasks.

(29) Overview of Education and Training (This should be a quick look at professional requirements. Please limit response to 12 lines of text.)

(30) Post Secondary Educational Programs: What do you see as the undergraduate majors which would be most desirable for persons who wish to be successful in graduate programs of library science in the next decade? Please list up to 8 majors.

(31) Graduate Programs in Library Science (Include here a general description of the typical content and requirements of graduate programs in Library Science.)

Appendix B
Original SIGI Text and Suggested Revisions

Definition of occupation? (Give any major divisions/groupings. Also give major employment areas --e.g. industry, academia, etc.)

Existing Text:
A professional, trained to acquire and manage library materials--books, newspapers, magazines, films, records, microfiche, computerized data bases. Helps people use library resources. May specialize in reference work (helping users to find information in specialized sources), acquisitions, cataloging, circulation, children's activities, computerized information retrieval, or particular subjects.

Suggested Revision:
A professional who works with people and ideas and the technologies that link them. Collects, organizes, manages, retrieves and disseminates information and knowledge recorded in all formats. May specialize in reference work; selection of new library materials; automated systems; computerized information retrieval; instruction; organizing and indexing library resources; administration. Most work in institutional settings such as schools, colleges, universities, public libraries, business information centers, government agencies, database development companies, and research organizations, but some are independent information brokers.

Description of work activities?

Existing Text:
General librarian: orders, catalogs, organizes books, magazines, other library materials. Reference librarian: helps people locate materials and aids in research. School librarian: helps develop young people's interest in reading: teaches them to use resources. In small libraries may perform many tasks.

Suggested Revision:
Some librarians work constantly with library users, helping with information needs, lecturing, performing computerized database searches, creating instructional brochures and lists of resources to aid users in academic and recreational pursuits. Some deal primarily with library materials, selecting, organizing, indexing, developing systems to maintain records and to guarantee easy access to information by library users. Those in administration supervise staff, set priorities, make budgets, do long range planning, manage buildings. In

small libraries, librarians may perform all activities described. In large libraries they may specialize.

Work setting(s)? Indoor/outdoor? (Describe physical work settings, typical travel, and/or on-site visits, if appropriate.)

Existing Text:
Libraries of all sizes, audiovisual or learning resources centers.

Suggested Revision:
Most librarians work indoors in dry, well-lighted, climate controlled environments. They work in schools, zoos, hospitals, colleges, prisons, corporations, government agencies, museums. A library can hold from several hundred books to several million - or hold no books at all, only films or sheet music or videos. Some librarians free-lance and work from home or private offices. Others spend much of their time teaching in classrooms. Travel to meetings, workshops, speaking engagements or distant research locations can be a large part of some positions.

Special problems/satisfactions? (Give the pros and cons of working in this occupation.)

Existing Text:
Evening or weekend hours required in some libraries. Patience needed to deal with the public. May need to stoop, lift or reach to high places for books.

Suggested Revision:
Offers daily opportunities for learning and for helping others in meaningful, satisfying ways: may turn a child on to reading; teach a student research skills needed to succeed in college; draw a diverse community together through creative programming. Libraries are often fast-paced, demanding work environments. This can be stressful, but is always challenging and invigorating. And it can be great fun. Rapid technological changes make continuing education vital. Since many libraries are open nights and weekends, flexible schedules are often available. Librarians are often asked to juggle a variety of demands for services, but given limited resources.

Specific Occupational training? (Include traineeships, practice teaching, residencies, etc.)

Existing Text:
Volunteer or do part-time work at a local library or in your college library while in school. Graduate library training programs often include work experience.

Suggested Revision:
Internship programs, field practicums and graduate assistantships are part of many graduate library education programs and are extremely helpful as a career start. Some post-graduate residencies are available. School library media specialists are often required to do student teaching in a library media center and sometimes also in a subject area.

Personal qualifications?

Existing Text:
Love of books, reading, and people. Must enjoy organizing, planning and handling details. Must be resourceful, tactful, and helpful. Able to speak and write clearly.

Suggested Revision:
Intellectual curiosity; pleasure in learning; commitment to service; intense belief in education and literacy for all; avid reader; ability to organize and synthesize information; good memory; an innovative problem solver who can move quickly from one activity to another. Strong communication skills both written and oral; patient and tactful when dealing with community of users; persistent and resourceful when doing research.

Appendix C
Revised SIGI Text

Definition of occupation? (Give any major divisions/groupings. Also give major employment areas --e.g. industry, academia, etc.)

Existing Text:
A professional, trained to acquire and manage library materials--books, newspapers, magazines, films, records, microfiche, computerized data bases. Helps people use library resources. May specialize in reference work (helping users to find information in specialized sources), acquisitions, cataloging, circulation, children's activities, computerized information retrieval, or particular subjects.

Suggested Revision:
A professional who works with people and ideas and the technologies that link them. Collects, organizes, manages, retrieves and disseminates information and knowledge recorded in all formats. May specialize in reference work; selection of new library materials; automated systems; computerized information retrieval; instruction; organizing and indexing library resources; administration. Most work in institutional settings such as schools, colleges, universities, public libraries, business information centers, government agencies, database development companies, and research organizations, but some are independent information brokers.

ETS Revision:
Collects, organizes, preserves and provides access to materials containing information, ideas and works of creative imagination--literature, poetry, films, etc. May work primarily with users, materials or library systems and computer software. May be employed in school system, public library, college/university library or special library containing limited range of materials. Special libraries are found in professional schools, research institutions, corporations, publishing houses, government agencies, law firms, etc. A few librarians are self employed.

Special problems/satisfactions? (Give the pros and cons of working in this occupation.)

Existing Text:
Evening or weekend hours required in some libraries. Patience needed to deal with the public. May need to stoop, lift or reach to high places for books.

Suggested Revision:
Offers daily opportunities for learning and for helping others in meaningful, satisfying ways: may turn a child on to reading; teach a student research skills needed to succeed in college; draw a diverse community together through creative programming. Libraries are often fast-paced, demanding work environments. This can be stressful, but is always challenging and invigorating. And it can be great fun. Rapid technological changes make continuing education vital. Since many libraries are open nights and weekends, flexible schedules are often available. Librarians are often asked to juggle a variety of demands for services, but given limited resources.

ETS Revision:
Public, college and university librarians may increasingly be frustrated by insufficient funds to maintain past levels of acquisitions and services. Satisfaction from helping people obtain information they need, encouraging reading among different populations, and bringing library services to those who cannot visit the library. Unlimited opportunities for learning. Much routine work now done by computers.

Examples of college courses?

Existing Text:
Liberal arts or science major: broad general background: one foreign language recommended: computer science. LIBRARY SCHOOL: cataloging theory, general and special reference services, computer applications to library procedures (e.g. searches), library management and administration (budgets and acquisitions): courses in special fields for special libraries, information science.

Suggested Revision:
Virtually any undergraduate major can provide a sound basis for a career in librarianship if it is accompanied by broad personal interests, intellectual curiosity and a commitment to pursue a graduate degree in library science. College courses recommended for all majors include: at least one foreign language, introduction to computers and computing, statistics, communications. School library media specialists also take education courses, including teaching methods and curriculum design.

ETS Revision:
English composition, communications courses, statistics, introduction to computers, one or more foreign language and broad background in humanities recommended. LIBRARY SCHOOL: cataloguing theory, general and special reference services, computer applications to library procedures, library

management and administration (budgets and acquisitions), courses in special fields for special libraries, information science. NOTE: School librarians usually required to take education courses and may do graduate work in any of several fields. Check your state.

Most important skills? (with examples of how they are used) (All skills listed below are considered ESSENTIAL in the occupation. You may add or delete from the listing, but if you add, (a) do not exceed 10, (b) select from the taxonomy of skills that follows the listing, and (c) be sure to give SPECIFIC examples of how they are used. You may use part of a skill--e.g., just "training" instead of "training, instructing.")

Existing Text:
SKILL #1: **Supervising, Directing**
Direct library assistants in preparation of catalog cards; supervise filing of information in card catalog or computer; oversee care of rare books and other valuable library materials.

Suggested Revision:

SKILL #1: SUPERVISING, DIRECTING, ASSESSING
Supervise personnel, students, support staff, and/or other professionals; direct programs, activities and work flows of a unit or of entire library; assess effectiveness of programs and services; evaluate personnel performances; prepare budgets and supervise expenditures of library funds; write reports detailing progress of unit or library.

ETS Revision:
Supervising, Directing
Direct library assistants entering catalogue information into computer, or preparing and filing catalogue cards; oversee care of valuable items in rare book collections; restrain children from running around and making too much noise; supervise intern from library school.

Other requirements? Experience? (Includes certification, licensure, continuing education, etc.)

Existing Text:
Certification requirements are set by states and differ widely. Education courses are often required for public school librarians. Special libraries may require master's degree in subject of library's specialization. Knowledge of computers is increasingly necessary. Continuing education courses available.

Suggested Revision:
Continuing education is necessary to keep up with current developments in the field and to update skills. Certification requirements are set by states and by some professional associations and differ widely. Education courses are often required for school library media specialists. Special libraries may require a degree in subject of library's specialization. Knowledge of and ability to use computers is essential. Foreign language skills are often a plus for working with certain materials and populations.

ETS Revision:
Certification requirements are set by states and professional associations. They vary widely--check state where you will work. Continuing education necessary to keep up with developments in the field and to update skills.

How do earnings vary?

Existing Text:
Salaries vary by supervisory level, amount of responsibility and technical skill required, geographic location, size, type of library, and years of experience.

Suggested Revision:
Salaries vary by geographic location, type of library, size of organization, supervisory level, amount of responsibility, technical skill. For academic librarians, pay varies with type of school and rank of position. In some schools and community colleges earnings vary by education level, degrees earned. Considerable variation by region in earnings of self employed practitioners. Highest paying functions are executive/administrative and computer/systems/automation related positions.

ETS Revision:
Vary by geographic location, type of library, size of organization, supervisory level, amount of responsibility, technical skill. Earnings of academic librarians vary with type of college/university and academic rank. In some two-year colleges, earnings vary with level and type of degrees. Highest paying positions are administrative and those concerned with computers, systems and automation. Librarians in K-12 schools typically earn less than those elsewhere, but do not work in summer.

Contribution to society?

Existing Text:
A great amount.

Suggested Revision:
A great amount: Librarians not only collect, organize, and preserve the recorded knowledge of humankind, they also provide access to that world of ideas and information and promote its use by all. Library services are essential to the work of writers, researchers, students and scholars. Librarians supply information needed for business, leisure, recreation, economic development, consumer choices and citizen participation in the political process. Access to information is crucial in a democratic society. Librarians contribute to the creation and maintenance of a literate, informed electorate.

ETS Revision:
A great amount: Preserves our heritage by keeping a storehouse of recorded knowledge. Encourages reading among people of all ages and conditions. Provides expert research services and instruction in search techniques.

Independence on the job?

Existing Text:
More than average: Some routine tasks. But administrators plan new programs and services, subject to approval of boards of directors.

Suggested Revision:
A great amount: As in most professions, independence grows with experience. Librarians may work at various levels of responsibility and within a broad framework of policies, but all are expected to use professional skills and judgement without close supervision. Academics plan their own lectures and choose their own research topics. Administrators create, plan and implement new programs and services subject only to guidance from boards of directors or trustees. Information brokers and consultants are most often self employed and are therefore completely independent.

ETS Revision:
More than average: Some routine tasks. But plans special programs and offers new services subject to approval of boards of directors.

Editor's Note
The author sent similar information to DISCOVER, an interactive career guidance tool published by ACT. The revisions, with very minor changes, were incorporated into the 1992 edition of DISCOVER.

Interests and Skills of Librarians as Measured By the Campbell Interest & Skill Survey

Richard W. Johnson, Dianne L. Nilsen, and David P. Campbell

The Campbell Interest and Skill Survey (CISS) is a new instrument for assessing the interests and self-rated skills of people in a wide variety of occupations including librarians.[1] It provides scores on four sets of interest and skill scales--the Orientation, Basic, Occupational, and Special scales--all of which can be helpful in describing the characteristics of librarians.

The Orientation scales measure interests and skills in seven general categories (e.g., helping, creating) that account for the primary ways in which people differ from each other in terms of interests and skills. The Basic scales divide the 7 general fields into a total of 29 specific interests and skills. For example, the Creating Orientation field is represented by Art/Design, Performing Arts, Writing, International Activities, Fashion, and Culinary Arts Basic scales. The Occupational scales show the degree to which one's interests and skills resemble the interest and skill patterns of people employed in various occupations. The Special scales measure psychological characteristics related to career planning, such as sociability, academic inclination, and breadth of interests and skills.

The CISS includes 200 items to assess one's interests in different activities and 120 items to evaluate one's self-confidence in various tasks. The interest items are answered on a six-point scale ranging from *Strongly Like* to *Strongly Dislike*, while the skill items are responded to by means of a six-point scale extending from *Expert* ("widely recognized as excellent in this area") to *None* ("have no skills in this area").

During the course of constructing the Occupational scales for the CISS, it was administered to representative samples of people in 58 occupations, including librarians. The data collected for this project provide a comprehensive profile of the interests and self-rated skills of librarians. These data are reported below.

Sample

The two librarian scales are based on the responses of a sample of 92 professional librarians (78 women and 14 men) who volunteered to participate in the scale construction process. These librarians were employed in a variety of settings including college libraries, community libraries, medical libraries, public school libraries, and other organizations. In general, their duties included assisting patrons (21-40% of time), reviewing and ordering materials (0-20% of time), maintaining materials (0-20% of time), administrative duties (0-20% of time), and other activities (0-20% of time). Eighty-five percent of the sample held advanced degrees (master's or doctoral degrees). The majority belonged to the American Library Association.

Orientation and Basic Scales

The mean CISS scores for the librarians that formed the occupational criterion sample are listed in the Appendix. The scores for the seven pairs of CISS Orientation interest and skill scales are shown in the left-hand column. (All of the scores are expressed as T-scores, that is, as standardized scores with a mean of 50 and a standard deviation of 10 based on the normative sample.) As indicated in the Appendix, the librarians scored highest on the Creating Orientation scales and lowest on the Adventuring Orientation scales. Curiously, they also scored relatively low on the Influencing and Helping Orientation scales, both areas that involve working with people.

The 29 Basic scales are listed in the middle column of the Appendix according to their Orientation category. As can be noted by reading the Appendix, the librarians scored high (T-score > 54) on the Writing and International Activities Basic interest and skill scales, both scales in the Creating area. They also scored above average (T-score > 52) on the Art/Design and Animal Care interest scales, the Culinary Arts and Office Practices skill scales, and the Plants/Gardens interest and skill scales. They scored low (T-score < 46) on the Athletics/Physical Fitness Basic interest scale and the Public Speaking and Military/Law Enforcement Basic skill scales. They scored below average (T-score < 48) on a number of Basic scales especially in the Influencing, Helping, and Adventuring areas.

Occupational Scales

The CISS Occupational interest and skill scales are listed in the right-hand column of scales in the Appendix. Because of the high scores obtained by librarians on the Creating scales, and also because scores on the Librarian scales were highly correlated with scores on the Creating scales, the Librarian interest and skill scales are classified as Creating occupations on the CISS profile. This type of classification agrees with primary classification of librarians as Artistic occupations on both the Strong Interest Inventory[2] and the Career Assessment Inventory.[3]

The Librarian Occupational scales consist of items that significantly differentiated between the interests and skills of librarians and the interests and skills of men and women in general. The Occupational interest scale contains 9 positively-weighted items (items for which librarians reported a higher degree of liking than did the average person) and ll negatively-weighted items (items for which librarians reported a higher degree of disliking than did the average person). The positively-weighted items focus on writing and literature; the negatively-weighted items suggest that, in general, librarians have a strong desire **not** to work with children or with angry, upset people. The Occupational skill scale contains nine items for which librarians report more skill than do people in the General Reference Sample. These nine items indicate strong skills in writing, research, and foreign languages, and a keen knowledge of classical music and historical events. Interestingly, all but one of the items found on the skill scale for librarians are also found on the skill scale for Academic Focus (described below).

As expected, librarians obtained their highest scores on the Librarian interest and skill scales. They also obtained high scores (T-score > 54) on other Creating occupations, notably Translator/Interpreter, Liberal Arts Professor, and Writer/Editor. In addition, they received high scores on the Psychologist interest scale and Secretary skill scale. They obtained low scores (T-score < 46) on a number of Influencing (e.g., School Superintendent, CEO/President), Helping (e.g., Nursing Administrator, Child Care Worker), and Adventuring (e.g., Athletic Coach, Athletic Trainer, Emergency Medical Technician, Military Officer, Police Officer, and Fitness Instructor) Occupational scales.

Research with the Librarian scales indicated that the interests and skills of librarians are not as sharply differentiated from the General Reference Sample as are the interests and skills of people in most occupations. For most occupations, the mean scores on the Occupational interest and skill scales were about two standard deviation units higher for people in the occupation than they were for people in general. However, the mean scores of librarians on the interest and skill scales differed by only 1.4 and l.3 standard deviation units, respectively, from the mean scores obtained by individuals in the General Reference Sample. In this regard, the librarians resembled public school teachers, retail store managers, and bookkeepers who do not show as distinctive interest and skill patterns as do most occupational groups.

Special Scales

The CISS also contains three pairs of special scales that can be used to describe the interests and self-rated skills of librarians (see bottom section of the Appendix). Academic Focus, the first of these pairs, consists of interest and skills items that distinguished between individuals in highly educated occupations and individuals in the remaining occupations in the General Reference Sample. Scores on these scales correlate highly with years of formal education. The average scores of the librarians on both the Academic Focus interest and skill scales were high (T-scores > 54). As such, the librarians can be expected to feel comfortable in college or university settings and to enjoy intellectual activities and discussions.

In contrast with the Academic Focus scales, scores on the Extroversion interest and skill scales were somewhat below average (T-scores < 48). These scales consist of items that correlate highly with measures of extroversion based on observations of others well acquainted with the subjects. High scores on these scales indicate that the person possesses extroverted traits such as outgoingness and sociability. The relatively low scores obtained by the librarians on the Extroversion interest and skill scales suggests that they are probably most comfortable working alone or in small groups and that they prefer activities where they can succeed primarily through solitary efforts.

The third pair of Special scales, the Variety interest and skill scales, indicate the range of one's interests and skills. Every one of the CISS interest items is scored on the Variety interest scale; every skill item is scored on the Variety skill scale. The T-scores obtained by the librarians on the Variety interest and skill scales (mean T-scores = 49 and 48, respectively) were just slightly below average. In general, they possess the same breadth of interests and the same degree of self-confidence as does the typical person in the General Reference Sample.

Summary

In summary, information acquired during the course of constructing the CISS Librarian scales shows that a representative sample of librarians possessed the following characteristics:

1. They expressed high interest and confidence in their skills for creative activities, especially writing and international activities. To a lesser extent, they also liked artistic tasks and caring for animals, reported confidence in their ability to do office work and to prepare food, and said that they both liked and performed well in horticultural activities.

2. They did not like adventuring activities, nor did they think that they could perform well in such activities (e.g., athletics/fitness, military/law enforcement, risk/adventure). In addition, they obtained relatively low scores for both their interests and their skills in mechanical crafts and in people-oriented activities such as public speaking, leadership and child development.

3. Their interest and skill patterns were similar to those of people in creative occupations including translators, liberal arts professors, and writers. They also shared the interests of psychologists and claimed skills similar to those of secretaries. The interest and skill patterns for the librarians were not as sharply differentiated from people in general as they were for people in most other occupational groups.

4. The librarians' interests and self-rated skills were similar to those of people who enjoy and pursue graduate study. Their CISS scores also indicated that they preferred solitary activities and lacked confidence in their social skills despite the large amount of time that they spend working with people.

REFERENCES AND NOTES

1. David P. Campbell, Susan A. Hyne, and Dianne L. Nilsen, *Manual for the Campbell Interest and Skill Survey* (Minneapolis: National Computer Systems, 1992).
2. Jo-Ida C. Hansen and David P. Campbell, *Manual for the SVIB-SCII*, 4th ed. (Stanford, CA: Stanford University Press, 1985).
3. Charles B. Johansson, *Manual for Career Assessment Inventory: The Enhanced Version* (Minneapolis: National Computer Systems, 1986).

Appendix

Mean Scores of Librarians on the Campbell Interest and Skill Survey

Orientation Scales	Basic Scales	Occupational Scales	Scores Int	Scores Skl
Influencing			**46**	**45**
	Leadership		47	46
	Law/Politics		48	49
	Public Speaking		47	45
	Sales		48	46
	Advertising/Marketing		50	48
		Attorney	47	49
		Financial Planner	47	45
		Hotel Manager	47	47
		Manufacturer's Representative	47	44
		Marketing Director	48	46
		Realtor	46	44
		CEO/President	45	45
		Human Resources Director	50	43
		School Superintendent	43	43
		Advertising Account Executive	54	48
		Media Executive	52	45
		Public Relations Director	53	47
		Corporate Trainer	51	45

Orientation Scales	Basic Scales	Occupational Scales	Scores Int	Skl
Organizing			**48**	**50**
	Supervision		47	48
	Financial Services		48	48
	Office Practices		50	54
		Secretary	50	56
		Bank Manager	46	46
		Insurance Agent	45	47
		Retail Store Manager	47	47
		Hospital Administrator	46	44
		Accountant	46	50
		Bookkeeper	49	50
Helping			**47**	**46**
	Adult Development		51	48
	Counseling		49	47
	Child Development		47	47
	Religious Activities		48	48
	Medical Practice		48	47
		Child Care worker	44	45
		Guidance Counselor	47	44
		Religious Leader	49	49
		Teacher K-12	51	47
		Social Worker	50	43
		Psychologist	55	47
		Nursing Administrator	44	43
Creating			**56**	**55**
	Art/Design		54	51
	Performing Arts		52	52
	Writing		55	58
	International Activities		55	55
	Fashion		52	51
	Culinary Arts		52	54
		Commercial Artist	55	50
		Fashion Designer	53	50
		Liberal Arts Professor	57	56
		Librarian	63	60
		Musician	56	52
		Translator/Interpreter	60	57
		Writer/Editor	55	54
		Restaurant Manager	51	52
		Chef	56	52

Orientation Scales	Basic Scales	Occupational Scales	Scores Int	Skl
Analyzing			**50**	**51**
	Mathematics		49	50
	Science		52	51
		Physician	51	48
		Chemist	53	51
		Medical Researcher	52	50
		Math/Science Teacher	51	50
		Computer Programmer	48	54
		Statistician	52	50
		Systems Analyst	51	52
Producing			**51**	**49**
	Mechanical Crafts		47	46
	Woodworking		50	47
	Farming/Forestry		51	51
	Plants/Gardens		54	54
	Animal Care		53	51
		Carpenter	51	45
		Electrician	47	44
		Veterinarian	53	50
		Airline Mechanic	48	46
		Agribusiness Manager	50	49
		Landscape Architect	52	49
		Architect	54	49
Adventuring			**44**	**44**
	Athletics/Physical Fitness		45	47
	Military/Law Enforcement		46	43
	Risks/Adventure		47	46
		Police Officer	45	37
		Military Officer	42	42
		Ski Instructor	49	42
		Test Pilot	46	44
		Athletic Coach	41	38
		Athletic Trainer	41	41
		Emergency Medical Technician	44	42
		Fitness Instructor	45	45
Special Scales				
	Academic Focus		56	55
	Extroversion		47	46
	Variety		49	48

ABBREVIATIONS: Int = Interest Scales Skl = Skill Scales

Orientation Scales	Basic Scales	Occupational Scales	Scores Int	Scores Skl
Analyzing			50	51
	Mathematics		49	50
	Science		52	51
		Physician	51	48
		Chemist	58	51
		Medical Researcher	52	50
		Math\Science Teacher	51	50
		Computer Programmer	48	54
		Statistician	52	50
		Systems Analyst	51	52
Producing			51	49
	Mechanical Crafts		47	46
	Woodworking		50	47
	Farming/Forestry		51	51
	Plants\Gardens		54	54
	Animal Care		53	51
		Carpenter	51	45
		Electrician	47	44
		Veterinarian	53	50
		Airline Mechanic	48	46
		Agribusiness Manager	50	49
		Landscape Architect	52	49
		Architect	54	49
Adventuring			44	44
	Athletics/Physical Fitness		45	47
	Military/Law Enforcement		46	43
	Risks/Adventure		47	46
		Police Officer	45	37
		Military Officer	42	42
		Ski Instructor	49	42
		Test Pilot	46	44
		Athletic Coach	41	38
		Athletic Trainer	41	41
		Emergency Medical Technician	44	42
		Fitness Instructor	45	45
Special Scales				
	Academic Focus		56	55
	Extroversion		47	46
	Variety		49	48

ABBREVIATIONS: Int = Interest Scales Skl = Skill Scales

Section II

1992 National Study

INTRODUCTION TO SECTION II

In early 1991, President-Elect Anne Beaubien of the Association of College and Research Libararies (ACRL) placed high priority on updating the vocational profiles of library and information professionsls. Beaubien and Mary Jane Scherdin, project manager, successfully wrote grant proposals seeking funding for the project. Success came in the form of monetary support from three organizations: the Association of College and Research Libraries, the American Library Association, (ALA), Office of Library Personnel Resources, and Consulting Psychologists Press. Margaret Myers, Head of the Office for Library Personnel Resources, served as ALA's liaison to Scherdin for the planning and implementation of the project. Later, ACRL Initiative Grants were awarded in order to fund further analysis of the data.

The following three chapters describe the study, with the first chapter explaining the results of the demographic questions, and the following two describing the results of the Strong Interest Inventory and the Myers-Briggs Type Indicator. A copy of all questions can be found in an appendix following the first chapter. For ease, the study will be referred to as the ACRL study, and library and information professionals will be referred to as librarians throughout the three chapters..

Statistical analyses were performed by Todd Michael Franke, formerly of the University of Wisconsin-Madison and currently Assistant Professor, School of Public Policy and Social Research, University of California, Los Angeles.

Several statistical tests were used to analyze the data. To help in understanding the data, graphs and descriptive statistics were employed. Categorical variables were analyzed using the Pearson's chi square test. For tables larger than 2 by 2, post hoc comparisons were performed following a significant omnibus test. When appropriate measures of associations were calculated, phi was used for 2 by 2 tables and Cramer's V was used for larger tables.

A general linear model approach was used to analyze the continuous variables. These ranged from t tests to factorial analysis of variance. When appropriate, post hoc comparisons based on Tukey or Scheffé's procedure were employed.

Simultaneous regression analysis was used to examine the effect of multiple independent variables on the dependent variables of interest. In the regression analyses, a dummy coding scheme was employed for all categorical variables. All analyses used an alpha level of .05.

In addition, Myers-Briggs data was analyzed using the Selection Ratio Type Table (SRTT) program written originally for Isabel Myers. This program compares the ratio of the number of people in each of the 16 types to the number that would normally be expected in each type. The SRTT software program used by Mary Jane Scherdin in this study was written by J. Glenn Granade, Harold H. Hatfield, Steven S. Smith, and Jacquelyn Beasley and published by the Center for Application of Psychological Type in 1987. It incorporates Chi-square and Fisher's exact probability.

From Children's Books to CD-ROMs: Life for Librarians Today

Mary Jane Scherdin

Background of Study

Just as the Association for College and Research Libraries (ACRL) began its effort to update the librarian profile on vocational interest inventories, Consulting Psychologists Press (CPP) was beginning its major revision of the Strong Interest Inventory. Because of ACRL/ALA's offer to participate and provide partial funding for this project, CPP decided to include librarians in its revision process. A total of 36 occupations were re-sampled and 11 new occupations added by CPP. Other occupations sampled included computer programmers, registered nurses, veterinarians, social workers, accountants, speech pathologists, bankers, lawyers, farmers, biologists, and actuaries.

During 1991 a research version of the Strong as well as a demographic questionnaire were developed by CPP. Some questions, such as age and years of experience, were used uniformly by CPP for all occupations. Other questions, specific to the library and information field, were constructed with the aid of the ACRL Task Force on Vocational Interest Inventories and were sent only to librarians. A copy of the demographic questions can be found in the Appendix. Questions 14-38 are librarian-specific questions, and all others are general questions asked of all occupations.

CPP's requirements for eligibility are set up with the purpose of finding a sample group that is representative of people in each occupation. Participants must be at least 25 years old, must be satisfied with their work, and must have been employed in the field at least three years. In addition, their job tasks must be typical for their occupation. A minimum of 200 men and 200 women who meet these criteria must complete the Strong inventory and the demographic questionnaire in order to generate a profile for each occupation.

The Myers-Briggs Type Indicator (MBTI®), a widely used personality and career guidance tool, is also published by CPP. The MBTI® gives information, such as communication patterns, ways of taking in information, and decision-making styles. Recent surveys reveal that the Strong and the MBTI® are among the most frequently used instruments by career counselors in colleges and universities.[1] Following discussion with the Research Coordinator at CPP, it was decided to use both instruments in order to gain as much information as possible about librarians. The Expanded Analysis Report (EAR) version of the MBTI® was chosen because it gives more detailed information about personality traits.

The sample group was composed of members of the two largest library associations in the United States, ALA and SLA (Special Libraries Association). A sizable sample was desired in order to obtain large enough subgroups to analyze differences among various specialties in the field. The sample of 3,500 represented 5.5% of the total memberships of ALA and SLA.

From SLA's membership of approximately 13,000, 750 names were selected on the basis of every 17th person. Students, retired persons, and members from Canada were excluded from the sample.

The total membership of ALA in 1992 was about 52,000. Because ALA collects and encodes additional demographic information in its membership database, it was possible to exclude persons who do not have typical job tasks:

unemployed/retired
trustees
self-employed and consultants
library school faculty
library school students
those working for a library association
anyone doing non-library work, such as publishers and vendors

In order to give the opportunity to compare ALA leaders with the general membership, two separate samples were drawn from the membership roster. First,

1,375 names were drawn from the 4,252 officers and committee members of the association. Then 1,375 were selected from the remaining 28,549 members. In terms of being representative of the ALA membership, this method of sampling clearly gives more weight to the officers and committee members, 32% of whom were sampled vs. 5% for general members. The rationale for this is that leaders of the profession are an important determinant of the direction the field is going.

Table 1
Sample

Group I	1,375 ALA Officers and Committee Members
Group II	1,375 ALA Members
Group III	750 SLA Members

TOTAL	3,500

Project Logistics

In March 1992, Strong Interest Inventories and demographic questionnaires were mailed to the sample of 3,500 persons. An accompanying letter printed on ACRL stationery and signed by Anne Beaubien, ACRL President, explained the project. She asked for cooperation in a unique opportunity to contribute to the profession by gaining an accurate understanding of the characteristics of librarians. They were told that their participation would give important information needed to update the librarian profile on vocational interest inventories and to guide prospective applicants into the field. In addition, participants were told that their individual results would be mailed to them, and that these results were confidential.

Because of the risk of one instrument biasing the other, CPP requested that participants complete the Strong and the MBTI® at least one week apart. Therefore the MBTI® was mailed out to each participant only after his/her Strong and demographic questionnaire had been received.

Responses

After data clean-up, there were 2,030 usable responses for the Strong Interest Inventory and the demographic questionnaire, a 58% response rate. The response rates broken down by group were:

Group I	*N*=851	64%
Group II	*N*=786	58%
Group III	*N*=366	48%

Of these, 1,697 had master's degrees in library and information science/studies (MLIS) and were satisfied in their work. This latter group was studied most intensely in the analyses, although responses from those with master's degrees who indicated dissatisfaction were also studied for comparison purposes.

A total of 170 did not have MLIS degrees and were not included in data analysis:

Group I	*N*=28 (3% of the group)
Group II	*N*=84 (11% of the group)
Group III	*N*=58 (16% of the group)

After excluding those without MLIS degrees and those who were dissatisfied, the make-up of the sample was as follows:

Table 2
Sample of Satisfied Librariens with MLS or MLIS

Group I	*N*= 770	45%
Group II	*N*= 655	39%
Group III	*N*= 272	16%
TOTAL	*N*=1,697	100%

Some who completed the Strong and demographic questionnaire did not complete the MBTI.® A few wrote to say that they had taken the MBTI® before and did not wish to take it again. There were 1,887 usable MBTI® responses, 1,600 from participants who had MLIS degrees and expressed satisfaction with their work.

In comparison to other occupations, the high response rate (58%) from librarians was a gratifying surprise to researchers at CPP. There were 379 questions on the research version of the Strong, 56 demographic questions, and 131 questions on FORM EAR of the MBTI.® Completing these 566 questions represented a significant commitment of time! A return of 30-35% is usually expected by CPP.

Demographic Information

In Tables 3-15 and 18-22, breakdowns are shown for specialties within the field for the group of 1,697 who met the following criteria: completed the Strong and the demographic questionnaire, had MLIS degrees, and were satisfied with their work. Even though CPP did not include those with less than three years experience in their analysis, these participants were included in the ACRL study. One of the author's objectives was to analyze differences between those who have recently entered the profession and those who have worked in the field for many years.

Throughout this chapter it is important to remember that not every participant answered every question; thus total responses may not always equal the total number in the sample.

Participants were asked to choose one of five specialties in which they spent the majority of their time. Results are found in Table 3.

Table 3
Type of Work

DOMINANT SPECIALTY	PERCENT	NUMBER
Technical Services	14%	228
Public Services - Adult	31%	517
Public Services - Children	12%	206
Administration	38%	644
Automation	5%	83
TOTAL	100%	1,678

Significant differences were found between Groups I, II and III on the number in each specialty. Almost half of Group I spent the majority of time in Administration (49%), while the highest percentages for Groups II and III were in Public Services - Adult (32% and 41%, respectively). It is interesting to note that administrators are represented so heavily in the ALA leadership positions (Group I). Administrators were also well represented in the other two groups, with Group II having 27% and Group III 35%. Group I had only 9% in Children's Public Services compared to 20% in Group II. Both Groups I and II had only 4% in Automation, while Group III had 12%. See Table 4.

Table 4
Type of Work by Group

	Group I	Group II	Group III
Tech Services	12%	16%	11%
Pub Serv-Adult	26%	33%	41%
Pub Serv-Child	9%	21%	1%
Administration	49%	27%	35%
Automation	4%	4%	12%
TOTAL	100%	101%*	100%

*error due to rounding

Participants were also asked to name the type of library in which they worked. Table 5 shows the breakdown of responses.

Table 5
Type of Library

PRIMARY EMPLOYER/ PLACE OF PRACTICE	PERCENT	NUMBER
School (K-12)	9%	143
Public (city, county, regional system)	30%	501
Academic	41%	685
(2 year vocational 3%)		
(4 year 38%)		
Special	13%	215
(profit 8%)		
(nonprofit 5%)		
Other	8%*	140
(State library agency 3%)		
(U.S. government 4%)		
(Network, Bibliog. util 2%)		
TOTAL	101%*	1,684

*errors due to rounding

To determine if the subgroups shown in Table 5 were representative of the ALA membership, a comparison was drawn between the size of the subgroups and the size of memberships in ALA divisions in 1992.

*Association of College and Research Libraries (ACRL)=9,536

*Public Library Association (PLA)=6,584
*American Association of School Librarians (AASL)=6,335

In the present study as well as in the ALA divisions, academic librarians (ACRL) were the largest of the groups. However, even though the school library division (AASL) was about the same size as the public library division (PLA), their frequency in Table 5 is less than one-third of that of the public librarians. It is possible that not as many school librarians are ALA officers or committee members, since it is more difficult for them to take time off during the school year to attend committee meetings at Midwinter conference. Thus, there were probably fewer school librarians eligible for the sample of this study. Table 6 shows the make-up of Groups I, II and III by type of library.

Table 6
Type of Library by Group

	Group I	Group II	Group III
K-12 School	5%	16%	0%
Public	31%	39%	4%
Academic	53%	36%	18%
Special	2%	5%	65%
Other	10%	4%	13%
TOTAL	101%*	100%	100%

*rounding error

Reasons for Engaging in Librarianship

One uniform question addressed to all occupations being studied was "I am engaged in this occupation because:". Participants could mark as many of the answers as applied. Table 7 shows how librarians responded to this question.

The question regarding reasons for engaging in this occupation and the multiple choice answers were uniform for all occupations and could not be modified for librarians. However comparisons can be drawn with previous studies of the library profession.

Moen and Heim's 1988 study of library school students showed agreement with the present study in the students' reasons for choosing the profession. The highest was clearly "intellectual opportunities," possibly comparable to both #1 and #2 above, followed by "service orientation," comparable to #3. Among the lowest were salary, benefits, and status, comparable to #6 and #7 above. Incidentally, the lowest by far was "routine work," a choice not listed as an option in the current study.[2]

Table 7
Reasons for Engaging in Occupation

ACTIVITY	PERCENT	NUMBER
1) I like to perform the activities it requires	87%	1,481
2) I can use my best talents	75%	1,275
3) I can make an important contribution	64%	1,093
4) I can use my training	63%	1,075
5) The working conditions (e.g. hours, supervision, vacations, or location) are desirable	57%	970
6) I can earn a good income	41%	691
7) People tend to respect it	22%	370
8) I fell into it by chance and have never left	16%	273
9) I stand little risk of failure	6%	96

(Percentages add up to more than 100 due to multiple responses)

There was also some similarity to White and Macklin's findings when studying 3,500 library school students in 1969. Their four highest requirements for the ideal job were related to intrinsic job satisfaction: 1) opportunity to use their particular knowledge and skills (comparable to #2 in Table 7); 2) opportunity to "really be myself," 3) opportunity to tackle challenging problems (comparable to #3 in Table 7); and 4) opportunity to do something creative. White and Macklin found very low ratings given to extrinsic rewards like money and prestige (comparable to #6 and #7 in Table 7).[3] In the ACRL study, a 41% response rate on #6, "I can earn a good income," seems to indicate that salary is more important than in the past.

When comparing the results of the ACRL study with that of Alice Bryan's study of public librarians in 1948,[4] similarities as well as differences were found. The largest percentage of participants in Bryan's study had entered the library profession rather than another career because they found the work interesting and enjoyable - similar to #1 above. The next highest percentage said that they doubted they had sufficient ability to succeed in other careers, a reason similar to #9 above, the reason chosen least often in the ACRL study. The explanation for this difference may be found in the time period during which Bryan's study was done. Many careers had not yet opened up to women. Therefore, if a woman did not have the inclination to be a nurse or teacher, she may have chosen the library field.

Pauline Wilson explored the concept of "drifting" into the field in her 1982 study. (This concept is similar to #8 in Table 7.) She stated that this phenomenon is typical of humanities majors since such preparation is often difficult to translate into a career outcome. "Not only is drifting into occupations common among humanities-trained people, it also characterizes their undergraduate years. They are more likely to change majors while in undergraduate school....The library profession probably acquires some very good drifters in the process."[5]

In the ACRL study, significant differences on reasons for being in the library field were found between librarians who work in various specialties and in different types of libraries. Tables 8 and 9 show percentages for groups that had contrasts.

Public services librarians ranked high on liking to perform the activities required for their jobs. Children's public services librarians most often stated they can use their best talents, and they can make an important contribution. Technical services have the most desirable working conditions; administrators have the least desirable. Automation specialists stated that they earn good incomes, and they think people tend to respect the profession.

Special for-profit librarians were least likely to feel they were making an important contribution, but they were highest on stating that they can use their training. School and community college librarians ranked highest on desirable working conditions. Public librarians were least satisfied with their incomes.

U.S. government librarians most often stated they fell into the field by chance, while special for-profit and school librarians were least likely to state this as a reason for being in the field. School librarians usually must obtain a degree in education, including a student teaching component, as well as take library and information courses; thus it would be difficult to drift into this type of library by chance.

Analysis by years of experience revealed significant differences between those who had been in the profession less than 5 years, 6-10 years, and more than 11 years. The greatest disparity was found on the following responses: I can earn a good income, People tend to respect it, I fell into it by chance and have never left, I can make an important contribution, and I can use my best talents. In each of the five cases, the number of people who checked the responses rose with length of experience.

Table 8
Comparisons of Reasons Engaged in Occupation by Type of Work

Significant differences and percent who responded to each reason:

	Children's Public Services	Adminis-trators	Adult Public Services	Technical Services	Automa-tion
"I like to perform the activities it requires."	91%	84%	92%		
"I can use my best talents."	83%		71%	72%	
"I can make an important contribution."	75%			56%	
"I can use my training."					
The working conditions are desirable."		52%		64%	
"I can earn a good income."			33%		55%
"People tend to respect it."	18%			17%	28%
"I fell into it by chance and have never left."					

Significance is at the .05 level or better on Chi Square analysis.

Table 9
Comparisons of Reasons Engaged in Occupation by Type of Library

Significant differences and percent who responded to each reason:

	Network/ Bibliographic Utility	Special For-profit	Special Non-profit	US Government	K-12 School	Public	Community, Junior College, Vocational, Technical	University/ College
"I like to perform the activities it requires."								
"I can use my best talents."								
"I can make an important contribution."	81%	47%						
"I can use my training."		74%	55%	53%				
"The working conditions are desirable."	41%				71%		72%	
"I can earn a good income."	56%	57%		56%		34%		
"People tend to respect it."								
"I fell into it by chance and have never left."			10%	30%	9%			

Significance is at the .05 level or better on Chi Square analysis.

Professional Memberships

Some participants were members of both ALA and SLA. Although Group III, the SLA portion of the sample, makes up 16% of the total sample, 20% of the total respondents stated they belong to SLA. Likewise, although the combination of Groups I and II make up 84% of the sample, 89% stated membership in ALA.

Analysis of the responses of the groups showed that more SLA members belonged to other national associations than did ALA members. On the other hand, more ALA members than SLA members belonged to regional, state and local associations - 78% to 47%.

Those who have worked in the field more than 11 years were more likely to belong to regional, state and local library associations (78%) than those who have worked 6-10 years (65%) or those who have worked 0-5 years (66%).

Certification

School library media certification is held by 17% (*N*=294) of the total sample, but only 9% or 143 are currently working in K-12 schools. Public library certification is held by 29% (*N*=486), and 30% or 501 are currently working in public libraries. Medical Library Association certification is held by 2% (*N*=36).

Job Activities

Participants were asked to indicate how much of their working time was devoted to certain job activities. They were asked to choose None, 1-25%, 26-50%, 51-75% or 76-100% for each of 11 job activities. Table 11 shows the number of respondents who indicated they spent at least 25% of their time on each activity. Naturally, it is possible for persons to spend over 25% of their time on up to three different activities.

Table 10
Memberships in Professional Associations

ASSOCIATIONS	PERCENT	NUMBER
American Library Association	89%	1,513
Regional, state or local library association	75%	1,267
Special Libraries Association	20%	342
American Society of Information Science	4%	73
American Association of Law Librarians	3%	48
Medical Library Association	3%	48
Society of American Archivists	2%	30

(Percentages add up to more than 100 due to multiple responses)

Table 11
Job Activities

Those who spend more than 25% of their time on certain activities:

ACTIVITIES	PERCENT	NUMBER
1. Administration/Management	54%	907
2. Reference/Reader services	38%	632
3. Collection Development/Acquisitions	24%	411
4. Automation Planning/Designing/Coord	15%	247
5. Computerized Database Searching	14%	236
6. Group Activities/BI/Storytelling/Curric. Dev.	13%	216
7. Cataloging/Class/Indexing/Abstracting	11%	184
8. Publicity/Public Relations/Fund-raising	9%	157
9. Circulation/Collection Access/ILL	6%	107
10. Records Management/Archives	2%	39
11. Conservation/Preservation	2%	32

(Percentages add up to more than 100 due to multiple responses)

In Group I, 65% spent more than one quarter of their time on administration compared with 54% overall. The top three activities for Groups I and II are identical to those listed above. Members of Group III, however, spent most of their time on Reference/Reader Services, Administration/Management, and Computerized Database Searching (in rank order).

Work activities were analyzed by length of time in the profession: 0-5 years, 6-10 years, and over 11 years. The most dramatic differences were found in administrative activities and database searching. As expected, more experience in the field was related to more administrative activities. Those with more experience also spent more time on automation and on public relations activities. In contrast, those with less experience were more likely to spend their time on database searching, circulation/collection access activities, reference services, archives, and cataloging activities. These are tasks usually performed in entry level positions. In addition, those who have recently graduated from MLIS programs may have more training in database searching than those who have been in the field longer.

Analysis of the five major library specialties: technical services, adult public services, children's public services, administration, and automation, showed that there were only two specialties that did not decrease with years of experience - administration and children's public services. Children's public services includes both K-12 and public librarians. In contrast to other groups, it appears that they stay in their positions rather than moving into administration.

Higher percentages of special librarians were found in the groups with 0-5 and 6-10 years experience. This was particularly true of those in the nonprofit sector. This could mean that special librarians are leaving the profession or leaving their jobs in special libraries. The other possibility is that more positions have opened up in that area in recent years. On the other hand, school librarians had lower percentages in the groups with 0-5 and 6-10 years of experience and a higher percentage in the group with more than 11 years of experience. These librarians seem to be staying in their jobs, and possibly fewer positions have opened up in the last few years. The percentages of all other groups stayed approximately the same through the years.

Favorite Activity

When asked which activity they would choose to spend more time on, participants indicated Collection Development/Acquisitions and Reference/Reader Services as their favorite activities. See Table 12 for the rank order and number who chose each activity.

Table 12
Favorite Activity
(participants could choose only one)

ACTIVITIES	PERCENT	NUMBER
1. Collection Development/Acquisitions	18%	296
2. Reference/Reader Services	18%	293
3. Administration/Management	16%	256
4. Automation Planning/Designing/Coord	12%	199
5. Group Activities/BI/Storytelling/Curric. Dev.	10%	155
6. Publicity/Public Relations	8%	125
7. Computerized Database Searching	7%	114
8. Cataloging/Class/Indexing/Abstracting	6%	95
9. Conservation/Preservation	3%	51
10. Circulation/Collection Access/ILL	1%	17
11. Records Management/Archives	1%	16
TOTAL	100%	1,617

When comparing the rankings of those who performed an activity more than 25% of the time (Table 11) with those who chose that activity as their favorite (Table 12), Collection Development, Preservation, and Publicity/PR each ranked higher as favorite activities. However, Preservation was the only activity where the number of people who chose it as their favorite activity (*N*=51) was higher than the actual number presently performing the work more than 25% of the time (*N*=32).

Breakdowns of the three favorite activities by group, listed highest to lowest are:

Group I	Group II	Group III
Administration	Reference/Read Serv	Reference/Read Serv
Coll Devel/Acquis	Coll Devel/Acquis	Database Searching
Reference/Read Serv	Administration	Automation

The special librarians in Group III gave a higher rating to database searching and automation activities than the ALA members in Group I and II. Does this mean that they are more technologically oriented? As noted above, the librarians in Group III have been in the profession a shorter length of time, and this could account for some of the difference between groups.

Significant differences were found on favorite activities based on number of years experience in the profession. Those who had been in the field for five years or less tended to select database searching as their favorite activity, while their least favorite activity was administration. These librarians have most likely been trained recently in database searching and feel comfortable with it. The highest number of those who have been in the profession for 6-10 years chose cataloging as their favorite activity, and the lowest number chose administration. Those in the field less than 10 years probably have not yet had much experience in administration, and thus do not consider it a favorite activity. Those in the field for 11 years or more selected administration most often and cataloging/indexing least often. In a survey of library school students nine years after graduation, it was found that a significant number of librarians characterized themselves simply as administrators.[6]

Administrative Activities

When asked if they would enjoy management/administration as a component of their jobs, 84% said they would. (See Table 13.) Group I, nearly half of whom spent the majority of time in administration, recorded an even higher 87%, while a lower, but still substantial 78% of Group III expressed enjoyment of administrative activities. This is a major change from the results of earlier studies where librarians were portrayed as being weak in leadership qualities and lacking in desire to supervise.[7]

Similar to the selection of a favorite activity, there was a significant difference in the like and dislike of management activities based on length of time in the profession. Those in the field for five years or less were more apt to state a dislike for management, while those in the field for over 11 years tended to state they enjoyed the activity very much.

Table 13
Enjoyment of Administrative Activities

	PERCENT	NUMBER
Enjoy very much	53%	894
Enjoy somewhat	31%	522
Neutral	7%	115
Dislike somewhat	7%	122
Dislike very much	2%	35
TOTAL	100%	1,688

Computer Use

An impressive 97.5% of participants reported they use computers in their work (*N*=1,632). (See Table 14.) Thirty percent reported using computers during more than 50% of their work time. What may be even more surprising, 94% said they enjoy using computers. Less than 1% said they very much dislike using computers. There was no difference in these results when analyzed by years of experience in the profession.

Table 14
Use of Computers

	PERCENT	NUMBER
Enjoy using computers very much	69%	1,165
Enjoy somewhat	25%	426
Neutral	3%	58
Dislike somewhat	2%	39
Dislike very much	less than 1%	3
TOTAL	100%	1,691
Proportion of daily work involved with computers:		
None	3%	54
1-25%	39%	664
26-50%	28%	479
51-75%	20%	334
76-100%	10%	161
TOTAL	100%	1,692

The inclination for computer use is a major change from what was expected and predicted about the library profession. Librarians have been described as conservative, resistant to change, and low on technical interests.[8]

It has been my observation that librarians have been less resistant to technology than the general population, many of whom still prefer to curl up with a good book rather than a computer screen. Librarians have taken the lead with computers, continually training hesitant users to search online catalogs and CD-ROM databases.

Career Choice and Years of Experience

Sixty-two percent (N=1,044) said the library and information field was their first career. Analysis by group showed that there was a significant difference between groups on this question: 66% of Group I indicated it was their first career, 55% of Group II, and 62% of Group III. The implication is that ALA leaders made a commitment earlier in their lives to librarianship. As one might expect, there was also a significant difference by number of years in the profession. Those who have more than 11 years in the profession were more likely to say that the library profession was their first career choice (67%) than those who have 6-10 years (50%) and those with 5 years or less (43%).

In the ACRL study, 50% of the participants made decisions to enter the field by age 24, 80% by age 30. Average age was 25. Group II was higher (age 26) than the other two groups.

Moen and Heim, in their 1988 study of library school students, found that 30% had decided to pursue a master's degree after working in a non-library field. Only 17% had decided to pursue an MLS or MLIS before completing their undergraduate degrees.[9]

Similarly, Webb and Pearson's 1985 survey of 1,500 library school students found that 23% had chosen the library field before completing their undergraduate degrees.[10] In 1969, White and Macklin found that 23% of the library school students had chosen the library profession before age 20, 46% by age 24, and 70% by age 30.[11] These figures are approximately the same as those in the ACRL study.

Bryan found that 84% of the public librarians she studied in 1952 had chosen librarianship as a career before the age of 29, with a median age of 22.5. Forty-four percent made the choice between the ages of 20 and 24. An additional 25% chose the profession between ages 16 and 19 and another 15% between ages 25 and 29. Although the median age is much lower than the average age of 25 in the ACRL study, it is important to keep in mind that less than half of the librarians in Bryan's study had earned the first professional degree, i.e., one year beyond the undergraduate degree. As in the ACRL study, librarianship was a second career for 40% of librarians in Bryan's sample.[12]

Seventy-five percent of the sample from the ACRL study had at least 10 years experience in the field, with the average being 16 years. The average number for Group I was significantly higher at 18, while Group II and III were lower at 15. The average number of years spent in current jobs was eight with no significant differences between the groups.

Public View of Librarians
When asked how they thought the public views librarians, general responses were positive. However, only 13% stated that the public viewed librarians very positively, while 19% replied that the view was somewhat negative. See Table 15 for further information.

Table 15
Public View of Librarians

	PERCENT	NUMBER
Very positively	13%	219
Somewhat positively	67%	1,123
Somewhat negatively	19%	321
Very negatively	1%	19
TOTAL	100%	1,682

Group III, the special librarians, had the lowest percentage who thought the public's view was positive (68%), while Group I's positive response was 83% and Group II 80%. Librarians in Group I, most of whom are administrators, may have more interaction with other librarians or educators and may not have as much interaction with the general public. Special librarians work closely with a public who usually do not value intellectual activity as a top priority, as school and academic librarians do. Even public librarians usually work with a public who voluntarily seeks them out for their services. In a 1991 membership needs survey conducted by Ann Thompson, Director of Research for SLA, an open-ended question was asked regarding any topic area or issue in which members felt SLA should be fostering research. Two of the topics requested most often were: 1) measuring the value and status of the library and its staff within the organization, and 2) the image of librarians.[13] Even though there is a concern among librarians in many types of libraries regarding image, the question of value and status within the organization is probably more unique to special librarians.

Satisfaction
Two questions regarding satisfaction were asked in the demographic questionnaire, one about work in general (Question #11) and one about various aspects of the current job (Question #39). On the first question, participants could choose one of four responses: very satisfied, somewhat satisfied, somewhat dissatisfied, and very dissatisfied. Fully 93% of respondents indicated they were satisfied, considerably higher than the 79 to 85% found in other studies using the Strong Vocational Interest Blank.[14]

General dissatisfaction with their work was expressed by only 6% of both Groups I and II, while the figure was almost twice as high - 11% - for Group III, the special librarians. As noted above, Group III had the highest percent who said the public's view of librarians was negative. A regression showed that, in general, there was a strong correlation between satisfaction and a positive response to the question regarding the public's view of librarians.

There may be several reasons why special librarians express more job dissatisfaction. Special librarians in for-profit agencies work in a highly competitive atmosphere where they see many people making higher salaries and see no opportunity for advancement for themselves. The mission of the library is in the hands of the parent institution, and that institution is controlled by another profession usually having little in common with the lofty ideals of libraries. This atmosphere is probably not supportive for librarians, as expressed in their answers to the question regarding the public's view of them. In addition, half of SLA members work in libraries with five or fewer employees, and one-third have only a single professional. There is often little opportunity for professional development, a strong interest expressed by SLA members in the 1991 needs assessment survey.[15]

Using the question of general satisfaction, a multiple regression was carried out correlating satisfaction with factors that influence the selection of the library field. If a person had a positive response on certain questions, he or she was more likely to answer negatively on the general satisfaction question. It was found that the following factors were predictors of dissatisfaction:

*Engaged in profession to earn a good income
*Engaged in profession to use training
*Engaged in profession because there was little risk of failure

Conversely, the following factors were predictors of satisfaction, meaning that if a person had a positive response on these questions, he or she was more likely to be somewhat or very satisfied:

*Engaged in profession to use best talents

*Engaged in profession because people respect it
*Engaged in profession because like to perform activities
*Engaged in profession to make an important contribution

Significant differences were found on the general satisfaction question when comparing librarians by type of specialty as well as by type of library. Children's librarians had the highest percentage of satisfied respondents (98%). How ironic that these librarians are becoming an endangered species, when there is the greatest possibility of satisfaction.[16] In looking at the reasons for engaging in the library field, children's librarians were significantly higher in saying, "I can make an important contribution." (See Table 8.) They were also significantly higher in checking "I like to perform the activities it requires" and "I can use my best talents." However, they were among the lowest in saying that people tend to respect what they do. Is there a way, at least within the profession, to show children's librarians that they are respected and valued?

Technical services librarians, on the other hand, had the highest dissatisfaction rate (13%); automation librarians were a close second with 11%. Table 8 shows that technical services librarians were significantly lower in stating they can make an important contribution, they can use their best talents, and people respect what they do. If their skills are under-utilized in the library field, how can we make better use of them?

Automation librarians were also significantly lower in stating they can make an important contribution; however, they were significantly higher in saying that people tend to respect what they do and they can earn a good income. It should be noted that even though they had the highest percentages on the latter two items, they were still relatively low (28% and 55% respectively).

Correlations were also found between satisfaction and enjoyment of computers and enjoyment of management activities. Satisfaction was greater for those who enjoy using computers (93%), and dissatisfaction was as high as 18% for those who dislike using computers. Likewise, those who enjoy management activities had a 94% average on satisfaction, while those who dislike management had a dissatisfaction rate of 19%.

No significant differences in satisfaction were found based on the age a person decided to enter the profession or on the number of years experience in the field. It was found that females were more satisfied than males.

The second satisfaction question referred to the participant's present job only: "How satisfied are you with aspects of your current job?" The two highest-ranked satisfactions were job responsibilities and the opportunity to use skills and abilities. The highest dissatisfaction was with salary, followed by supervision/feedback and the opportunity for development and promotion. See Tables 16 and 17.

Table 16
Satisfaction with Current Job

Satisfaction with aspects of current job:
(Number of responses in parentheses)

	DISSATISFIED	NEUTRAL	SATISFIED
Working hours	**6%** (109)	**12%** (207)	**82%** (1,369)
Responsibilities	**4%** (54)	**11%** (177)	**86%** (1,453)
Opportunity to use skills and abilities	**4%** (66)	**10%** (173)	**86%** (1,443)
Opportunity for development and promotion	**17%** (282)	**25%** (426)	**54%** (974)
Supervision/feedback	**19%** (324)	**25%** (420)	**56%** (934)
Salary	**21%** (349)	**26%** (434)	**54%** (902)
People on your job	**5%** (84)	**19%** (323)	**76%** (1,275)

A comparison with Bryan's 1948 study shows little or no change from those in the ACRL study. Inadequate financial return and insufficient opportunity for advancement were the two most frequently checked reasons for dissatisfaction with library work.[17]

Table 17
Satisfaction with Current Job

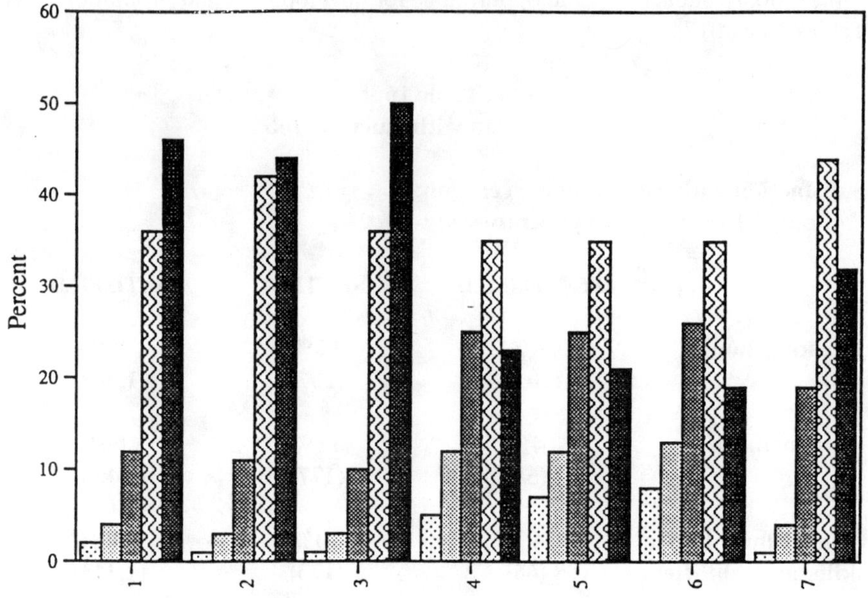

Aspects

1. Working hours
2. Responsibilities
3. Opportunity to use skills and abilities
4. Opportunity for development and promotion
5. Supervision/feedback
6. Salary
7. People on your job

Not Satisfied

Very Satisfied

A survey on career development conducted in 1984 for the Office for Library Personnel Resources found that the majority (82%) selected challenging/varied work as the most important factor in job satisfaction. Opportunities for growth/advancement ranked second. High salary ranked second to last. Least important was authority/influence over others. As many as 41% predicted they would not achieve their desired career goals. Obstacles were: 1) lack of available jobs (30%), 2) relocation concerns (22%), and 3) achieving financial security (13%). Respondents from the different library settings included in the sample (public, school, academic, and special) all ranked lack of available jobs as their primary concern. Special librarians appeared to be more concerned with achieving financial security. Eighty percent of all types of librarians said there were not good career opportunities at their workplace.[18]

Other Demographic Information

The sample for the ACRL study was made up of 78% females (*N*=1,318) and 22% males (*N*=379). Twenty years earlier, White and Macklin's survey showed 16% were male.[19] Moen and Heim's 1988 sample of library school students was comparable, with 19% male.[20] The average age was 45 for Groups I and II and 43 for Group III.

The three most common undergraduate majors in the ACRL study were language/literature, history, and education. These results were quite similar to Moen and Heim's top three of English/literature, education, and social science[21] and identical to White and Macklin's three highest, English, history and education.[22] There were differences in the ACRL study based on years of experience in the profession. The group who had entered the field less than five years ago had more degrees in biology, journalism, psychology and religion/philosophy than did those who had been in the field longer. The group who had been in the profession 6-10 years had more degrees in Law and Physical Science. Those in the field 11 years or more had more majors in art, education, history, and language/literature than did the other two groups. See Table 18 for more information regarding educational backgrounds.

Table 18
Educational Characteristics

7%	Hold a Ph. D. 5% of females, 14% of males 11% of Group I, 3% of Groups II & III
	Most common undergraduate degrees: 1) Language/Literature 2) History 3) Education
97%	Are either satisfied or very satisfied with their choice of a major
10%	Are currently enrolled in a course
55%	Would like to go back to school in the future

Almost 93% of the ACRL sample was Caucasian, similar to Moen and Heim's 94%. African Americans made up 3% of the ACRL sample and 4% of the Moen and Heim study of library school students.[23] See Table 19 for further information on ethnic background and nationality.

Tables 20, 21 and 22 report further demographic information.

Table 19
Ethnic Background and Nationality

ETHNICITY:	NUMBER
American Indian	5
Alaskan Native	5
Asian or Pacific Islander	27
Black	51
Caucasian	1,561
Hispanic	15
Other	17
TOTAL	1,681

English first language - 96% yes
English most commonly used language in home - 99% yes

How long speaking English		
	6-10 years	$N = 4$
	11-20 years	$N = 3$
	More than 20 years	$N = 1,650$

COUNTRY OF BIRTH:
95% U.S.
1% China
1% Germany
3% Other countries

HOW LONG LIVED IN THE U.S.	NUMBER
Less than 2 years	0
2-5 years	1
6-8 years	8
11-20 years	10
More than 20 years (99%)	1,626
TOTAL	1,645

Table 20
What Occupations Have You Frequently Daydreamed of Going Into?
(could choose 2)

50%	Writer, artist, entertainer, athlete (Actor, musician, painter, editor, ball player, etc.)
24%	Professor (college and university)
15%	Lawyer
11%	Executive, Administrator, Manager
9%	Medical practice
7%	Architect
	(lawyer and professor were reversed for Group III)

Table 21
What Activities Do You Enjoy When You Are Not Working?
(could choose 2)

HIGHEST CHOICES

50%	Reading
23%	Attending artistic events (art exhibits, theater, dance)
23%	Spending time with friends or family
19%	Nature related activities (hiking, camping, bird watching)
13%	Engaging in artistic activities (drawing, photography, theater, dance)
12%	Playing individual sports (golf, tennis, cycling)
12%	Gardening

LOWEST CHOICES

.2%	Watching individual sports
.3%	Playing team sports
.5%	Gambling
1.7%	Financial Activities
1.8%	Going to or hosting parties or dances
2.1%	Raising or training animals

Table 22
Other Characteristics of the Group of Satisfied Master's Degree Librarians Are:

Other characteristics of the group of satisfied master's degree librarians are:
78% female $N = 1{,}318$
Median age = 44

When growing up, mother's primary occupation:
61% homemaker
9% worker, operator
9% teacher (primary, secondary)

When growing up, father's primary occupation:
9% Sales proprieteor, supervisor, manager
9% Executive administrator, manager
7% Precision production, craft and repair occupations—worker
6% Precision production, craft and repair occupations—proprietor, supervisor, manager
6% Engineer, surveyor
5% Professor
5% Laborer

Marital Status:
64% married, 22% single, 2% widowed, 13% divorced/separated (rounding error)

Primary caretaker for any children living with you? 72% no

Primary caretaker for any adults living with you? 93% no

Do you have any physical disabilities? 96% no

Conclusion

Recruitment and retention of the finest work force is vital to the library and information profession. It is hoped that the information presented in this chapter will help to promote these two goals. Factors that influenced career choice as well as elements of satisfaction have been presented. Differences by type of library and type of specialty have been explored.

A strong correlation exists between librarian satisfaction and the public's view of and respect for librarians. Accurate information needs to be disseminated within as well as outside of the profession in order to attract and keep talented people who will be happy in their work.

REFERENCES AND NOTES

1. Allen L. Hammer and Jean M. Kummerow, *Strong and MBTI® Career Development Guide* (Palo Alto, CA: Consulting Psychologists Press, 1992), 1.
2. William E. Moen and Kathleen M. Heim, ed. *Librarians for the New Millennium* (Chicago: American Library Association Office for Library Personnel Resources, 1988), 104.
3. Rodney F. White and James Macklin, *Careers and Professionalization in Librarianship and Information Science* (Washington D.C.: U.S. Department of Health, Education, and Welfare, 1970), 21.
4. Alice I. Bryan, *The Public Librarian; A Report on the Public Library Inquiry* (New York: Columbia University Press, 1952), 127-29.
5. Pauline Wilson, *Stereotype and Status; Librarians in the United States* (Westport, Conn: Greenwood Press, 1982), 142-43.
6. Herbert S. White, "The Education and Selection of Librarians: A Sequence of Happenstances," *Library Journal*, 115 (October 15, 1990): 61-62.
7. See references in "Marian the Librarian" chapter in this volume regarding low interest in management/administrative activities: Bryan, Douglass, and Denis.
8. James M. Kusack, "Librarians and the Information Age: An Affair on the Rocks?" *Bulletin of the American Society for Information Science*, 14 (December/January 1988): 26-27. Kusack, "Librarians and the Information Age: Is Reconciliation Possible? *Bulletin of the American Society for Information Science*, 14 (February/March, 1988): 27-30. Jerry D. Campbell, "Choosing to Have a Future," *American Libraries* 24 (June 1993): 560-64. See also references in "Marian the Librarian" chapter in this volume: Clift, Presthaus, Fine, and Hamilton.
9. Moen and Heim, *Librarians*, 101.
10. T.D. Webb and Richard C. Pearson, "Generalist Training Won't Do," *American Libraries*, 17 (November, 1986): 780.
11. White and Macklin, *Education*, 14.
12. Bryan, *Public Librarian*, 61, 117, 120,.
13. Ann Thompson, "Special Libraries Association Membership Needs Assessment Survey," *Special Libraries*, 83 (Winter, 1992): 48.
14. David P. Campbell, *Handbook for the Strong Vocational Interest Blank* (Stanford, CA: Stanford University Press, 1971), 67.
15. Thompson, *Special Libraries*, 32, 42, 44.
16. Patricia Glass Schuman, "Strategies for Surmounting Navel-Gazing," *American Libraries*, 24 (November 1991): 1006.
17. Bryan, *Public Librarian*, 128-29.
18. Ellen Bernstein and John Leach, "Plateau," *American Libraries*, 16 (March 1985): 178-79.

19. White and Macklin, *Education*, 6.
20. Moen and Heim, *Librarians*, 96.
21. Ibid, 100.
22. White and Macklin, *Education*, 12.
23. Moen and Heim, *Librarians*, 99.

Appendix
Demographic Questions

1. Name

   ____

2. Gender: (mark one) _____Male _____Female

3. Age_______

4. What is the highest level of education that you have completed?
   ________Less than high school
   ________High school
   ________Trade/technical training
   ________Some college
   ________An Associate degree
   ________A Bachelor's degree
   ________A Master's degree
   ________A Professional degree (e.g., DDS, JD, MD etc)
   ________A Doctorate (e.g, PhD, EdD)

5. To answer the following question, please refer to the code sheet that contains the list of Educational Codes. Major(s) or primary concentration(s) in school:

   A____________ B____________

6. How satisfied are you with your choice of school major or concentration?
   ________I am very satisfied
   ________I am somewhat satisfied
   ________I am somewhat dissatisfied
   ________I am very dissatisfied

7. Fill in the name of your specific major or concentration in school:

   ____

8. Are you currently enrolled in any courses?
   ___________Yes
   ___________No

9. Would you like to go back to school in the future?
___________Yes
___________No

10. What is your exact job title?
____

11. How do you feel about your work? (Choose one)
___________I am very satisfied
___________I am somewhat satisfied
___________I am somewhat dissatisfied
___________I am very dissatisfied

12. Average number of hours per week you work in your position? (choose one)
_______Less than 10
_______Between 10 and 19
_______Between 20 and 29
_______Between 30 and 39
_______40 or more

13. I am engaged in this occupation because (Mark as many as apply)
__________I can use my best talents.
__________I can earn a good income.
__________People tend to respect it.
__________The working conditions (e.g. Hours, supervision, vacations, or location) are desirable.
__________I like to perform the activities it requires.
__________I can use my training.
__________I fell into it by chance and never left.
__________I can make an important contribution.
__________I stand little risk of failure.

Questions #14-38 (Librarian)
Overall, how much of your working time is devoted to each of the following activities? Use the following scale:

1 = None
2 = 1-25 percent
3 = 26-50 percent
4 = 51-75 percent
5 = 76-100 percent

14. Circulation/Access services/Interlibrary loan. (1)
15. Reference/Reader services/Information and referral. (2)
16. Computerized database searching. (3)
17. Group activities (e.g, curriculum development, instructional consultant, bibliographic instruction, storytelling). (4)
18. Collection development and management/Acquisitions. (5)
19. Cataloging/Classification/Indexing/Abstracting/Thesaurus construction. (6)
20. Records management/Archives. (7)
21. Conservation/Preservation. (8)
22. Automation planning, designing and coordination. (9)
23. Administration/Management. (10)
24. Publicity/Public relations/Fund-raising. (11)

25. In which one specialty area do you spend most of your time?
    (1) Technical Services
    (2) Public Services: Adult (including college)
    (3) Public Services: Children/Youth
    (4) Administration
    (5) Automation

26. What is your primary employer or place of practice?
    (1) K-12 school library
    (2) Public library (city/county/regional system)
    (3) Community college/junior college/vocational-technical school library
    (4) University/4-year college library
    (5) Special library in for-profit organization
    (6) Special library in non-profit organization (non-governmental)
    (7) State library agency
    (8) U.S. Government (including armed forces)
    (9) Network/bibliographic utility
    (10) Library association

27. Which of the following professional organizations do you belong to? (choose all that apply)
    (1) American Library Association
    (2) Special Libraries Association
    (3) American Association of Law Librarians
    (4) Medical Library Association
    (5) American Society for Information Science
    (6) American Society of Indexers
    (7) Society of American Archivists
    (8) Regional, state, or local library association

28. Which of the following certifications/licenses do you hold? (choose all that apply)
(1) School library media
(2) Public library
(3) Medical Library Association

29. If you could choose to spend more time on one work activity, which one would it be? (Choose one of the activities from items 14-24. Enter **one** code from the column to the right of the items.)

30. Do you hold a Master's degree in Library Science or Library and Information Science?
(1) Yes (2) No

31. Are you the MLS-degreed professional in your library?
(1) Yes (2) No (3) I do not have this degree

32a. Do you personally use computers in your work?
(1) Yes (2) No

32b. Does someone who reports to you or with whom you work very closely use computers?
(4) Yes (5) No

33. Do you/would you enjoy using computers in your work?
(1) Enjoy very much
(2) Enjoy somewhat
(3) Neutral/don't care
(4) Dislike somewhat
(5) Dislike very much

34. Approximately what proportion of your daily work involves the use of computers?
(1) None
(2) 1-25 percent
(3) 26-50 percent
(4) 51-75 percent
(5) 76-100 percent

35. Do you/would you enjoy having management/administration as a component of your job?
(1) Enjoy very much
(2) Enjoy somewhat
(3) Neutral/don't care
(4) Dislike somewhat
(5) Dislike very much

36. Is library and information your first career?
(1) Yes (2) No

37. If you answered No to question 36, what was your first career? (Use the **Occupational Codes** on the code sheet. Code 01-09 mark one digit only; codes 12 and above mark two digits on line 37.)

38. How do you think the public views librarians?
(1) Very positively
(2) Somewhat positively
(3) Somewhat negatively
(4) Very negatively

39. Using the following scale, how satisfied are you with the following aspects of your *current* job? (0=not satisfied 4=satisfied)
________Working hours
________Responsibilities
________Opportunities to use your skills and abilities
________Opportunities for development and promotion
________Supervision/feedback
________Salary
________People on your job

40. Number of years in your occupational field or line of work?__________

41. At what age did you decide to enter the field you are currently in?________________

42. Number of years experience at your current job?______________

To answer the following questions, please refer to the code sheet that contains a list of occupational codes.

43 When you were growing up, what was your mother's primary occupation?__________

44 When you were growing up, what was your father's primary occupation?__________

45. What occupations have you frequently daydreamed of going into? (choose one or two)_______________ _______________

46. Ethnicity
_______American Indian
_______Alaskan Native
_______Asian or Pacific Islander
_______Black
_______Caucasian
_______Hispanic
_______Other (Please specify)

47. Was English the language you learned first?
_______Yes _______No

48. Is English the language most commonly used in your home?
_______Yes _______No

49. How long have you been speaking English?
_______Less than 2 years
_______2-5 years
_______6-10 years
_______11-20 years
_______More than 20 years

To answer the following question, please refer to the code sheet that contains a list of Country codes:

50. What country or region were you born in? (country code for U.S. is 15).__________

51. How long have you lived in the United States?
_______Never lived in the U.S.
_______Less than 2 years
_______2-5 years
_______6-10 years
_______11-20 years
_______More than 20 years

To answer the following question, please refer to the code sheet that contains the list of leisure codes.

52. What activities do you enjoy when you are not working? (choose one or two). __________ _________

53. Marital Status
_____Married/Partnered
_____Single
_____Widowed
_____Divorced/Separated

54. Are you the primary caretaker for any children living with you?
________Yes ________No

55. Are you the primary caretaker for any adults living with you?
_______Yes _______No

56. Do you have any physical disabilities?
_______Yes _______No

AUTHOR'S NOTE: In question #31, the word "only" was inadvertently omitted before "MLS". Therefore the answers to this question were unable to be used in the study.

CODE SHEET

Educational Codes:
01. Accounting
02. Agriculture
03. Architecture
04. Art
05. Biological Science
06. Business
07. Business: Clerical

08. Computer and Information Sciences
09. Education
10. Engineering
11. History
12. Human Services (Cosmetologist, Law Enforcement Officer)
13. Journalism
14. Language/Literature
15. Law
16. Machine Trade
17. Mathematics
18. Medicine/Health Services
19. Music/Theater Art
20. Physical Science
21. Psychology
22. Religion/Philosophy
23. Social Science
24. Structural Work/Construction
25. Transportation
26. Vocational Technical
27. Other (Please Specify)

Occupational Codes:

PROFESSIONAL SPECIALITIES-

01. Architect
02. Engineer, Surveyor
03. Mathematician, Statistician, Actuary
04. Computer Scientist, Systems Analyst
05. Accountant, Auditor
06. Medical Practice (Physician, Dentist)
07. Medical Therapist (Physical, Speech)
08. Registered Nurse, Physician's Assistant
09. Professor (College and University)
10. Teacher (Primary and Secondary)
11. Counselor (Educational and Vocational)
12. Library and Information Professional
13. Lawyer, Judge
14. Social, Recreation, and Religious Work
15. Writer, Artist, Entertainer, Athlete
16. Agriculture, Forestry, Conservation, Food Science
17. Biological Sciences
18. Physical Science
19. Social Science

TECHNICAL SPECIALITIES
23. Computer programmer
24. Paralegal, Legal Assistant
25. Airplane Pilot, Air Traffic Controller
26. Health Technologist/Technician
27. Technologist/Technician other than Health

SALES OCCUPATIONS
28. Proprietor, Supervisor, Manager
29. Worker

ADMINISTRATIVE SUPPORT OCCUPATIONS
34. Supervisor
35. Worker, Operator

SERVICE OCCUPATIONS
36. Food, Household
37. Protective Service
38. Health Service
39. Personal Service (Barber, Child Care)

FARMING, FORESTRY, FISHING OCCUPATIONS
45. Proprietor, Supervisor, Manager
46. Worker

PRECISION PRODUCTION, CRAFT AND REPAIR OCCUPATIONS
47. Proprietor, Supervisor, Manager
48. Worker

TRANSPORTATION AND MATERIAL MOVING OCCUPATIONS
56. Supervisor, Manager
57. Worker, Operator

OTHER-
58. Executive/Administrator/Manager
59. Laborer
67. Homemaker
78. Other, please specify

Librarians in Transition: Profiles on the Strong Interest Inventory

Indra David and Mary Jane Scherdin

For more than a century librarians have struggled to overcome the unpopular image of their occupational stereotype that has been created by society and further augmented by the mass media.[1] To add insult to injury, several of the studies conducted on the profile of librarians over the years have indicated that the stereotype was not necessarily wrong. (Details are discussed in "Marian the Librarian" in this volume.) Career guidance inventories, such as the Strong Interest Inventory, are used to measure vocational interests of members of a particular occupation and develop profiles for each occupation. Are these profiles an accurate reflection of librarians, and if not, what can be done to change them?

The Strong Interest Inventory

Psychologists and vocational choice experts agree that personality traits have a bearing on occupational behavior, affecting both one's choice of and success in a particular occupation. Studies have often matched people's psychological and vocational needs, values, attitudes, personality traits, likes and dislikes with their choice of career and with job satisfaction.

The Strong Vocational Interest Blank was originally developed by E. K. Strong, Jr. in 1927 and became well established by 1943 when Strong wrote his seminal work on the vocational interests of men and women.[2] Strong believed that different groups of professional people showed consistent differences in what they said they liked and disliked. Some of these differences seemed reasonable, but other differences turned up on items having no apparent connection with jobs - such as types of people, hobbies, and non-vocational aspects of life. A profession may represent a way of life or a kind of life style as well as a way of earning a living.

John Holland developed a theory of vocational choice in the 1950's that was incorporated into the Strong inventory and has remained its underlying basis.[3]

Holland's theory has undergone a series of major and minor revisions and is among the most widely used by researchers and counselors alike.[4] His theory is based on the assumption that vocational interests are one aspect of what is commonly called personality, and that an individual's vocational interests match the work environment in which he or she will most likely be comfortable or satisfied.

Holland drew on more than 550 published studies to organize and classify occupations. He contended that people can be characterized by their resemblance to each of six personality types: Realistic, Investigative, Artistic, Social, Enterprising and Conventional or some combination of two or more of these, such as Realistic-Investigative.[5]

Over the years, the Strong inventory has been under systematic and continuous assessment. The latest version, known as the Strong Interest Inventory (SII), is one of the most highly respected vocational interest inventories. A review in the Mental Measurements Yearbook states that there has been more self-conscious concern for the quality of construction and development of the SII than for any other psychometric instrument.[6]

The SII is a measure of interests, not aptitude or intelligence, and is used chiefly as an aid in making long-range curricular or occupational choices. It compares an individual's interests, likes and dislikes with those of people employed in a wide variety of occupations. Each occupation is represented by a national sample of experienced, satisfied workers who are performing typical activities of that occupation.[7]

In its 1994 revision, the SII gives four main types of information:

1. scores on the six Holland types listed above, called the General Occupational Themes, which reflect the respondent's overall occupational orientation;
2. scores on 25 Basic Interest Scales, sub-divisions of the General Occupational Themes, which report interests and aversions in specific areas, such as art, science, and public speaking;
3. scores on 211 Occupational Scales, which indicate the degree of similarity between the respondent's interests and the characteristic interests of women and men in a wide range of occupations; and
4. scores on four Personal Style Scales that measure Leadership Style, Risk Taking/Adventure, Learning Environment, and Work Style.

Of the 211 Occupational Scales, most are matched-sex, i.e., each occupation has two scales, one for men and the other for women. In addition there are five occupations represented only by female scales (child care worker, dental assistant, dental hygienist, home economics teacher, and secretary) and two occupations represented only by male scales (agribusiness manager and plumber.)[8] It has been found that separate-sex scales are more valid, since men and women, on the average, do respond differently to almost half of the inventory items. Studies demonstrate that the route to equal treatment is not necessarily through identical treatment.[9]

Following are descriptions of the six Holland types or General Occupational Themes. Further information can be found in the Appendix.[10]

Realistic types have outdoor and technical interests. They prefer doing jobs that produce tangible results, operating or designing equipment or huge machines, and using tools that require manual dexterity. Typical occupations are mechanic, engineer, electrician, fish and wild life specialist, crane operator and tool designer.

Vocational preferences for *Investigative* types include doing scientific or laboratory work, solving problems through thinking, and collecting and organizing data. Occupations include astronomer, biologist, chemist, technical writer, zoologist, and psychologist.

Artistic types have dramatic, self-expressive interests. They like composing, writing, decorating, designing, and completing projects independently. Preferred occupations are artist, author, composer, writer, musician, stage director, and symphony conductor.

People in the *Social* category like to help others and have people-oriented interests. Teaching, coaching, leading discussion, and doing group projects appeal to these types. Occupations include social worker, teacher, guidance counselor, school administrator, recreation leader, and speech therapist.

Work activity interests for the *Enterprising* Theme are selling, purchasing, leading and managing people, managing projects, and chairing committees. Vocational preferences include business executive, political campaign manager, real estate salesperson, buyer, and retail merchandiser.

Typical work activities for *Conventional* types are scheduling, keeping records and financial books, making charts and graphs, and organizing and maintaining office procedures. Occupations include accountant, credit manager, business education teacher, bookkeeper, clerical worker, and quality control expert.

An occupation's complete profile would include characteristics of all six Themes, but codes are usually developed on the basis of the two or three most prevalent Themes. Thus, the Theme code SAE would describe a person who has Social, Artistic, and Enterprising interests, in that order. Although the SII assumes a score of 50 as the average score, usually a minimum score of 51 is needed on any one Theme before it is considered important enough to be used as part of the Theme code for a particular occupation.

Prior to the 1992 study co-sponsored by the Association for College and Research Libraries (ACRL), the American Library Association (ALA) Office for Library Personnel Resources, and Consulting Psychologists Press (CPP), the latest information on librarians was drawn from a 1977 survey of ALA members. At that time, librarians were placed in the Artistic category and given a code of "A". The scores on the other Themes were not high enough to be included.[11]

David's 1990 study of three groups of Michigan librarians, academic, automation, and online search services, also concluded that all three groups were dominant on the Artistic Theme, and not significantly different from the 1977 sample.[12] The chapter in this volume entitled "Marian the Librarian" provides further historical information on librarians' scores on the various versions of the Strong inventory as well as other vocational interest inventories.

Research Design and Methodology

A research design developed for the ACRL study is described in an earlier chapter in this volume, "From Children's Books to CD-ROMs." The goal of the study was to either validate the existing librarian profile or, if appropriate, to create a new profile for librarians.

The research version of the Strong Interest Inventory (SII) as well as the Myers-Briggs Type Indicator, and a demographic questionnaire were used to survey librarians in the study. CPP provided disks with scoring information, and the data was analyzed by staff under the direction of Mary Jane Scherdin. Data analysis methods are described in the Introduction to Section 2 of this volume.

Librarians were scored on the SII using the 1985 scoring norms, the latest available at that time. This means that they were compared with the 1985 General Reference Sample, i.e., scores of all persons who took the 1985 version of the inventory. In mid-1994, CPP completed its revision, compiled the new General Reference Sample, and supplied updated scores for librarians. A new manual, based on this revision, is to be published in late 1994 and will include the revised librarian scores. In this chapter, information will be given based on both the 1985 and 1994 reference samples.

For purposes of comparison in the ACRL study, the following sample groups were formed:

Group I	American Library Association officers and committee members
Group II	American Library Association members
Group III	Special Library Association members

Information was also collected from participants regarding type of library and specialty within the field.

The scores on the Strong Interest Inventory were analyzed to determine:

(1) Whether this sampling of the profession reflected a change in the profile of librarians by comparing them to people in general (the 1994 General Reference Sample of the SII) on the General Occupational Themes, Basic Interest Scales, Occupational Scales, and Personal Style Scales.

(2) Whether there were any significant differences between the three primary sample groups (Groups I, II and III), between librarian samples by type of specialty, and between librarian samples by type of library. (Scoring based on the 1985 General Reference Sample was used for these analyses.)

Types of libraries that were analyzed were school, public, special, academic (including community college), and "other." For purposes of this study, "other" includes state agency librarians, network and bibliographic utility librarians, and federal government librarians, including armed forces. Five types of specialties were analyzed: technical services, adult public services, children/youth public services, administration, and automation.

Results of the Study

A total of 2,032 usable responses (58% of the total sample) were sent to CPP for scoring, and 1,697 met the criteria for further analysis. The requirements were as follows: librarians with master's degrees in library science or library and information science who are satisfied with their work and whose work activities are typical of the field. CPP also requires participants to have a minimum of three years experience in an occupation in order to be part of the sample for that occupation. The ACRL study did not use the three-year requirement for two reasons: 1) it was felt that a person who has a master's degree and belongs to a national professional organization has demonstrated a sufficient commitment to the profession, and 2) comparisons were to be made between librarians based on number of years in the profession. Thus, the CPP sampling group was smaller than the group in the ACRL study, 1,542 vs. 1,697. In addition, the ACRL study used scores from dissatisfied librarians for purposes of comparison; however, these scores were not included in any other data analysis.

General Occupational Theme Scales

Table 1 displays average scores on the General Occupational Themes. These scores, based on the 1994 General Reference Sample, confirm previous findings that librarians are indeed dominant on the Artistic Theme. Both men and women scored highest on this Theme. Unlike most other occupations, they did not score over 51 on any other Theme.

Note that there are two scores for female and male librarians in Table 1. The separate scores are based on comparisons with others of the same gender in the General Reference Sample, while the combined scores are based on comparisons with the entire 1994 General Reference Sample, both male and female. For example, female librarians scored higher on the Realistic Theme when compared with other females than they did when compared with both genders (49.0 vs. 45.8). The combined average scores in Table 1 result from comparisons of the both male and female librarians with both genders in the General Reference Sample.

Table 1
Librarian Mean Scores On The General Occupational Themes
(Based on Separate Gender and Combined Gender Norms)

	FEMALE *N*=1,187		MALE *N*=355		COMBINED *N*=1,542
	Separate	Combined	Separate	Combined	
REALISTIC	49.0	45.8	44.1	47.6	46.2
INVESTIGATIVE	49.6	48.7	48.3	49.3	48.8
ARTISTIC	**54.0**	**56.3**	**56.8**	**54.1**	**55.8**
SOCIAL	47.6	48.8	48.1	46.9	48.4
ENTERPRISING	48.5	49.0	47.2	46.9	48.5
CONVENTIONAL	49.0	49.5	49.5	48.9	49.4

Holland's original placement of librarians was in the Conventional category, along with bank teller, bookkeeper, traffic manager and court stenographer. However, in subsequent studies this placement proved to be incorrect.[13] Librarians have been placed in the Artistic category since the mid-seventies, and the current ACRL study suggests that this designation has not changed since then.

The SII User's Guide reports that some people who score high in the Artistic category may be involved in the arts as spectators or observers rather than as direct participants. Their potential competencies include creativity, imagination and verbal-linguistic skills. They like to work in unstructured, flexible organizations that allow self-expression. Typical hobbies include reading, writing poetry or stories, collecting art work, and going to theatres, museums, and galleries. Artistic occupations include art museum director, artist, author-reporter, entertainer-musician, librarian, lawyer, advertising executive, and photographer.[14]

Following Artistic, the other scores cluster together closely and vary by the method of scoring. However, one of the highest scores for males, females, and the combined group is Conventional. It is interesting to note that the Artistic and Conventional Themes are normally considered incongruent, i.e., Artistic types tend to be nonconforming and original, while Conventional types prefer well-ordered activities. Although librarians' interests clearly fall in the Artistic Theme because of interests in reading, writing, music, art and language, the freedom and spontaneity characteristics of that Theme are tempered by the structured interests of the Conventional Theme. In addition, since computer and data management activities have been added as sub-divisions of the Conventional Theme, librarians' interests in this Theme might tend to be higher than in the past.

Another one of the highest scores for librarians is in the Investigative area. Female librarians scored higher on the Investigative Theme when compared only to other females than when compared to both genders. Parts of the description of the Theme seem quite appropriate for librarians, e.g., scholarly, analytical, curious, like to collect and organize data, and like to solve problems through thinking. Yet, librarians did not score high enough for this Theme to qualify as part of their Theme code. Most of the questions on the Investigative scale refer to science and mathematics. Given that there are few librarians with these backgrounds, it may be difficult for librarians to score high enough on this scale for it to become part of their Theme code.

Table 2
Percentage With Highest Scores on General Occupational Themes

THEMES	FEMALES	MALES
REALISTIC	12.9%	4.9%
INVESTIGATIVE	13.1	10.7
ARTISTIC	35.3	49.6
SOCIAL	11.4	9.6
ENTERPRISING	13.3	9.6
CONVENTIONAL	13.9	15.6
TOTAL	99.9%	100.0%
	(error due to rounding)	

A somewhat different perspective is given by looking at librarians' scores based on the number who scored highest on each one of the Themes rather than the average score for each Theme. Table 2 reports the percentages of females and males whose highest scores fell in each Theme scale (based on separate scoring norms). Similar to results in Table 1, a substantial percentage of female librarians scored highest on Artistic, and the other five scales were clustered very closely. Nearly half of the males scored highest on Artistic, with Conventional following at a distant second. Very few males scored highest on the Realistic Theme.

Significant Differences on the General Occupational Themes
Relationships were examined between groups based on type of library and type of work specialty. In the results below, significant differences are shown for pairs of sample groups on the General Occupational Themes. These differences were calculated based on the 1985 scoring norms.

1. No significant differences were observed between sample Groups I, II and III on the *Realistic Theme*. Differences were observed, however, between two librarian specialties; automation librarians showed more Realistic interests than children/youth librarians. Since automation specialists work with machines and technology, it seems appropriate for them to prefer the activities of this scale.

2. Group III (SLA members) was significantly higher than Group II (ALA members) on the *Investigative Theme*. Significant differences were also noted among various types of librarians; automation librarians, administrators, academic librarians, and "other" had more Investigative personality patterns than children's librarians and those working in public libraries.

3. All groups of librarians scored highest on the *Artistic Theme.* There were no significant differences between any of the groups.

4. Group III (SLA members) scored significantly lower than Groups I and II on the *Social Theme.* Other specialties with significant differences between each other on this scale are reported below:

HIGHER	LOWER
All groups	Technical Services
Children/Youth	Adult Public Services
Children/Youth	Administration
School Library	All groups except Public Library
Public Library	Academic/Comm. Coll. Lib.

5. As might be expected, Group I (ALA Officers and Committee members) scored higher than both Groups II and III on the *Enterprising Theme*, suggesting that ALA's leaders have more Enterprising interests than their colleagues. It was also found that there were slight but significant differences by specialty within each type of library. Public services librarians and administrators in public libraries showed more Enterprising personality patterns than their counterparts in academic libraries. Additional differences when comparing groups were:

HIGHER	LOWER
Administration	Technical Services
Children/Youth	Technical Services
Public Library	Academic/Comm Coll

6. Although Groups I, II and III did not differ on the *Conventional Theme*, some significant differences were observed between specialties. They are reported below:

HIGHER	LOWER
Administration	Adult Public Services
Administration	Children's/Youth
Automation	Children's/Youth
Admin Public Lib	Admin Academic Lib

Basic Interest Scales

Basic Interest Scale scores for male and female librarians were calculated using the 1994 scoring norms for the combined gender General Reference Sample. The top three interests for both genders included Writing, Art, and Music/Dramatics; all three are part of the Artistic Theme. A high score on the Writing scale indicates an interest in literature, reading, and language from the perspectives of both creation and appreciation. Other occupations that score high on this scale are: advertising executives, English teachers, lawyers, public relations directors, reporters, and writers.

Table 3 reports the high and low scores for male and female librarians. All scores above the mean of 50 are reported as high scores. In parentheses after each scale is the Theme with which it is associated, i.e., R=Realistic, I=Investigative, A=Artistic, S=Social, E=Enterprising, and C=Conventional.

The highest and lowest scores for librarians are similar to those from the 1977 librarian profile. At that time, the Writing and Music/Dramatics scales were highest and Athletics and Agriculture lowest.

Table 3
High and Low Scores on the Basic Interest Scales

HIGH SCORES (highest to lowest)

MALE		FEMALE	
Writing (A)	56.8	Writing (A)	57.4
Music/Dramatics (A)	53.4	Art (A)	55.7
Art (A)	52.7	Music/Dramatics (A)	55.6
Law/Politics (E)	52.5	Applied Art (A)	52.7
Public Speaking (E)	51.6	Culinary Arts (A)	52.7
Applied Art (A)	51.5	Office Services (C)	51.3
Religious Activ (S)	51.2	Computer Activ (C)	50.7
Science (I)	50.5	Nature (R)	50.5
Computer Activ (C)	50.4	Social Service (S)	50.4
		Merchandising (E)	50.1
		Religious Activ (S)	50.1

LOW SCORES (lowest to highest)

MALE		FEMALE	
Medical Service (S)	44.9	Athletics (R)	43.2
Agriculture (R)	45.4	Agriculture (R)	45.1
Athletics (R)	46.1	Medical Service (S)	45.4
Sales (E)	46.1	Military Activ (R)	46.3
Merchandising (E)	47.1	Mechanical Activ (R)	46.3

Significant Differences on the Basic Interest Scales

Using 1985 scoring norms, no significant differences were found based on type of library and type of work specialty on the following scales: *Agriculture, Nature, Military Activities, Medical Science* (now *Medical Service*), *Athletics,*

Office Practice (now *Office Services*), *Music/Dramatics, Art,* and *Writing* scales.

Significant differences were found between groups on the *Teaching* interest scale. Appropriately, school librarians and children's librarians scored higher than all other groups on this scale. In addition, adult public services librarians scored significantly higher than technical services. Adult public services personnel often spend a great deal of time on both formal and informal instruction in the use of the library.

The *Mechanical Activities* scale measures interest in activities that require working with machinery, large and small, e.g., computers. Not surprisingly, automation librarians scored the highest, while all librarians except those in technical services scored significantly lower.

Automation librarians scored highest on the *Science* scale followed by librarians who worked in state libraries, networks, consortiums etc. In addition, academic librarians scored significantly higher in this category than public librarians.

Significant differences were found on the *Mathematics* scale that measures an interest in working with numbers and performing statistical analyses. In general, academic and "other" librarians scored higher, while school and public librarians ranked lower on this scale. Children/youth librarians scored the lowest of all groups.

The *Social Service* scale measures interest level in helping and working with people. Comparisons between sample groups resulted in the following significant differences:

HIGHER	LOWER
Public Library	Academic/Comm. College
School Library	Academic/Comm. College
Children/Youth	All except Automation
Adult Services	Technical Services

In measuring interest level for *Religious Activities*, significant differences were found between children's librarians, who were higher than librarians in administration, and school librarians who were more interested in such activities than academic/community college librarians.

The *Law/Politics* scale measures the level of interest in debates and arguments designated to sell concepts rather than goods. Often associated with high scores in Public Speaking, members of occupations, such as lawyers and politicians, normally score high on this scale. Administrative librarians were the highest on this scale, differing significantly from technical services, adult public services, and children's librarians. The data also indicated that adult services librarians were significantly higher than technical services librarians, who scored lowest on this scale.

The *Public Speaking* scale measures an interest in persuading others through verbal activities, indicating a willingness to be in the limelight. Technical services librarians were least interested in this activity compared to others in the profession, and, as one might surmise, administrators had the highest scores. Librarians from special and academic libraries were less interested in public speaking than were those in public and school libraries.

There were significant differences between specialties on the *Merchandising* scale.

HIGHER	LOWER
Administration	Technical Services
Children/Youth	Technical Services
Administration	Adult Public Services
Public Library	Academic/Comm Coll
School Library	Academic/Comm Coll

The major difference between the *Sales* and the *Merchandising* scales is that people who score high on *Sales* like to take their product to others without prior invitation. Administrators scored significantly higher than all groups except children's librarians on *Sales*. Public librarians scored slightly but significantly higher than academic librarians.

Appropriately, administrators also scored the highest in expressing a preference for *Organizational Management* (formerly called *Business Management*), a scale that measures an interest in supervising, organizing, or directing others. There was also a significant difference between public librarians and academic/community college librarians on this scale, with public librarians scoring higher.

Two new scales, *Data Management* and *Computer Activities*, were added in this latest revision of the SII. *Data Management* involves managing financial, statistical, or mathematical data to provide assessments of decisions. *Computer Activities* directly measures interests in computers, computer science and office machines. Librarians scored means of 48.3 and 50.7, respectively, on these scales. Females scored 48.2 on Data Management and 50.7 on Computer

Activities; males scored 48.9 and 50.4, respectively. Because these scales were constructed so recently, statistical analyses comparing groups have not yet been performed.

Another new scale, *Applied Art*, is very similar to the *Art* scale. The subtle difference in the *Applied Art* scale comes from its broad emphasis on visual creativity and spatial visualization. Medical illustrators, architects and photographers show high interest on this scale. Most librarians scored above average, with males scoring 51.5, females 52.7, and the combined group 52.4.

Culinary Arts partially replaces the *Domestic Arts* scale which has been deleted from the 1994 revision. The new scale directly measures interests in cooking and entertaining. Librarians had a combined score of 51.7, with males scoring 48.3 and females 52.7.

Tables 4 and 5 present a summary of the significant differences on the General Occupational Themes and the Basic Interest Scales based on specialty and type of library.

Table 4
Differences in Librarian Scores by Type of Library

ACADEMIC LIBRARIANS:
- Higher on Investigative, Science, Mathematics
- Lower on Social, Enterprising, Social Service, Religious Activities, Public Speaking, Merchandising, Sales, Business (Organizational) Management

PUBLIC LIBRARIANS:
- Higher on Social, Enterprising, Social Service, Public Speaking, Merchandising, Sales, Business (Organizational) Management
- Lower on Investigative, Science, Mathematics

SCHOOL LIBRARIANS:
- Higher on Social, Teaching, Religious Activities, Public Speaking, Merchandising
- Lower on Science, Mathematics

SPECIAL LIBRARIANS:
- Lower on Public Speaking

"OTHER" LIBRARIANS:
- Higher on Investigative, Science, Mathematics

Table 5
Differences in Librarian Scores by Type of Specialty

ADMINISTRATIVE LIBRARIANS:

Higher on Enterprising, Conventional, Adventure, Public Speaking, Law/Politics, Merchandising, Sales, Business (Organizational) Management

Lower on Social, Religious Activities

AUTOMATION LIBRARIANS:

Higher on Realistic, Investigative, Conventional, Mechanical Activities, Science

CHILDREN'S/YOUTH PUBLIC SERVICES LIBRARIANS:

Higher on Social, Teaching, Social Service, Religious Activities

Lower on Realistic, Investigative, Conventional, Science, Mathematics

TECHNICAL SERVICES LIBRARIANS:

Lower on Social, Enterprising, Teaching, Social Service, Public Speaking, Law/Politics, Merchandising

ADULT PUBLIC SERVICES LIBRARIANS:

No significant differences

Occupational Scales

Except for the Librarian Occupational Scale itself, librarians did not have average scores higher than 50 on any other scale. In other words, there are no occupations that obtained indications of high interest from librarians. However, they did score over 40 on the following scales:

FEMALES		MALES	
Translator	46.6	Translator	44.4
Technical Writer	46.6	Paralegal	41.7
Flight Attendant	43.4	Lawyer	41.3
Speech Pathologist	42.4	Technical Writer	41.3
Musician	42.1	College Professor	40.8
Paralegal	42.0	Geographer	40.4
Medical Records Tech	42.0		
Advertising Exec	40.6		

The score of 40 was an arbitrary cut-off selected by the authors, and it should be noted that female librarians scored 39.9 on the Lawyer scale and 39.6 on the College Professor scale.

Personal Style Scales

Work Style

The Work Style scale differentiates those who like to work with people from those who prefer to work with data, ideas or things. (This scale was formerly called the Introversion/Extroversion scale. It is similar but not identical to the Extraversion/Introversion scale of the Myers-Briggs Type Indicator, which determines whether the focus and source of a person's energy is in the inner or outer world.) Scores of 55 and above tend to reflect a direction toward working with people, while scores of 45 or below show an interest in working with data, ideas or things.[16]

Librarians' average scores based on comparisons to the total 1994 General Reference Sample are as follows: males 46.9, females 50.8, and combined average 49.9. These scores indicate librarians are very near the mean of 50, thus reflecting a balance of interests in data, ideas, things, and people. Scores for males, although tending more toward interest in data, ideas, or things, still fell within the mid-point range. These findings are noteworthy, considering that many earlier studies tended to portray members of the profession as not being interested in working with people.

Learning Environment

The Learning Environment scale, formerly called the Academic Comfort Scale, in not a measure of ability but is designed to measure interest in intellectual exercises and comfort in an academic environment. The scale is normed so that occupational samples composed of people who have doctoral degrees score about 56-65; those with professional degrees such as dentists, lawyers and optometrists score 50-55; those with master's and bachelor's degrees score 45-55; those with two-year degrees score 35-44; and people with high school diplomas tend to score 34 or lower.

High scores on this scale indicate an orientation towards theoretical and research problems, and low scores indicate an orientation towards practical and applied problems. Occupations with Investigative or Artistic interests tend to score in the upper range (50-55), whereas occupations with more practical and applied interests in the Social or Enterprising areas usually score in the lower range (45-50).[17]

Librarians, as an occupational group, scored exceptionally high with a mean score of 56.6. Males scored slightly higher than females, 57.3 and 56.5, respectively. In the 1994 General Reference Sample, females with doctoral degrees had a mean of 57.8, and males had a mean of 56.

Even though numerous activities in the library world have been considered practical in nature, many of those tasks are now being taken over by computers. Librarians are more frequently taking on higher level theoretical and research activities, and the scores show this to be very appropriate.

Leadership Style
A recently developed scale is that of Leadership Style. Librarians scored a mean of 50.8, with males and females having almost identical scores. Scores on the Leadership Style scale do not measure interest in becoming a leader per se, but rather they indicate a liking or a disliking of activities that are associated with active, directive, take-charge behaviors. The scale contrasts those who are outspoken in their views with those who may be reluctant to assume active leadership roles that require them to be directive. The latter may lead by example or be very effective "behind the scenes" or leading self-managed work teams. Librarians' scores at the mid-point indicate a balance between directing others and leading by example.

Risk Taking/Adventure
The fourth Personal Style Scale, Risk Taking/Adventure, was formerly one of the Basic Interest Scales. The mean score for librarians was 45.3, with males scoring 48.1 and females 44.4. Administrative librarians were more willing to take risks than any other group of librarians. Usually males and younger people score higher on this scale, because it involves physical risk-taking activities.

Librarian Differentiation from General Population
The Tilton overlap, an analysis that indicates how clearly one occupation is differentiated from the general population, resulted in significant differences for librarians.[18] Male librarians are separated from the 1994 General Reference Sample of men in the SII samples by 1.6 standard deviations; female librarians are differentiated from the General Reference Sample of women by 1.29 standard deviations. For some perspective, a separation of two standard deviations corresponds roughly to differences of 30 IQ points or 6 inches in height.

Certain scale items differentiated librarians from others in the General Reference Sample, and these are called Most and Least Predictive Items. These are items where there was the greatest amount of difference between the librarians' scores and the General Reference Sample. The Most Predictive Items are those questions which librarians answered more positively ("like") than others who weren't librarians, and the Least Predictive Items are those questions that librarians answered more negatively ("dislike") than those who weren't librarians. Table 6 reports the Most and Least Predictive Items for male and female librarians in rank order. There are strong similarities between males and females - seven of the ten items are identical.

Table 6
Most and Least Predictive Items for Librarians

FEMALE LIBRARIAN SCALE ITEMS

Five most predictive:

- art museum director
- author of novels
- city planner
- editor
- foreign services officer

Five least predictive:

- competitive sports
- play team sports with friends
- outside work vs. inside work
- physical activity vs. mental activity
- physical education director vs. free-lance writer

MALE LIBRARIAN SCALE ITEMS

Five most predictive:

- art museum director
- author of novels
- editor
- foreign correspondent
- foreign services officer

Five least predictive:

- outside work vs. inside work
- physical activity vs. mental activity
- physical education director vs. free-lance writer
- have mechanical ingenuity (inventiveness)
- enjoy tinkering with small hand tools

Years of Experience

In order to see if there were differences on the General Occupational Themes based on years of experience in the field, the total sample of librarians was divided into three groups:

Low, with 0-5 years professional experience, (*N*=188)
Medium, with 6-10 years in the profession (*N*=252)
High, with 11 or more years of experience (*N*=1,250)

Preliminary statistical analysis based on the 1985 scoring norms showed slight but significant differences between groups in three of the Theme scales. Librarians with "Low" number of years experience in the profession scored higher on the Investigative scale than those with a "High" level of experience. Librarians in the "Medium" group scored higher on the Realistic scale than those in the "High" group. On the other hand, librarians who have been in the profession over 11 years tended to score higher on Enterprising than those in the other two groups. The difference in the "High" group might be explained by the fact that administrators score higher on Enterprising, and there are more administrators in the group with 11 or more years of experience.

Occupational Satisfaction

Is there any relationship between satisfaction in the field and the General Occupational Themes? The SII survey asked whether the participants were very satisfied, somewhat satisfied, somewhat dissatisfied or very dissatisfied with their work. A regression analysis revealed that there was a correlation between higher scores on the Conventional Scale and higher levels of job satisfaction. On the other hand, there was a correlation between higher scores on the Enterprising Scale and lower levels of satisfaction with librarianship. Those who score high on the Enterprising Theme tend to dislike the long periods of intellectual effort that would be needed in libraries. In addition, low salaries could be a cause of discontent.

Summary and Conclusions

The general purpose of this study was to ascertain the extent to which the vocational interests of librarians had changed over the years. When analyzing the scores of librarians on the General Occupational Themes and the Basic Interest Scales, statistical comparisons indicated that although there were some significant differences between the three main samples, Groups I, II and III, and between the specialties within the field, all were clearly dominant on the Artistic Theme. Scores on the other Themes were close together, showing a balance of interests in many areas.

The results of the survey have some implications for the profession even though the Theme code of A (Artistic) has not changed in recent years. Career counselors using the SII must be made aware that librarianship will be a more satisfying occupation to those who are able to balance their interest in working with people and their interests in working with data, ideas and things. They should be comfortable in an academic environment. Beyond that, librarians have a variety of interests, including writing, art, music, science, foreign services, computer activities, social service, religious activities, and even merchandising, public speaking, and law/politics. What a diverse group of interests!

Library school faculty may wish to use the results of the comparisons between types of specialties to help guide students into concentrations within the field. This information suggests areas where librarians will feel comfortable, maximize their potential, and find satisfaction. The profession may be able to retain good librarians who might otherwise become dissatisfied and leave the field.

More data is needed on school librarians, who were under-represented in this study. The American Library Association estimates that they make up approximately 45% of librarians in the United States. However, the figures are approximate, since the data includes "librarians & media" as one group, and it is impossible to separate librarians from other professionals working in school media centers.[19] In addition, many school librarians have degrees in the education field and do not have master's degrees in library and information studies, one of the requirements for the ACRL study. Still, they are prominent members of the library field and do have a great deal of influence on the public's image of librarianship. It is hoped that a study of school media specialists will be undertaken in the future.

With the advent of the Information Age and the emphasis on the information professional, librarianship has begun to attract people with higher Investigative interests. This study found that those who have been in the field a shorter period of time manifested a slight but significantly higher interest in Investigative activities. It is Scherdin's belief that a new Basic Interest Scale, which would be a sub-division of the Investigative Theme, should be developed. This scale is needed in order to cover the area of general inquiry. The scale would include activities of occupations such as lawyers, journalists, and librarians, all of whom do research and investigation into information on a wide variety of subjects. As mentioned above, currently the Investigative Theme covers mainly science and math. An important element of the Information Age is missing and needs to be incorporated in the Investigative Theme.

By the year 2014 most of the 44-year-olds in the profession (mean age of librarians in this study) would have retired and those in this study who have less than five years of experience may be at the peak of their careers. It will be interesting to test librarians in the profession again 15-20 years from now and compare them with librarians in this study.

In concluding this chapter, it is important to note that there are many encouraging signs of change in the public's image of librarians. David relates an anecdote that occurred during the sixth ACRL conference in Salt Lake City. During a cab ride, she was chatting with the young driver and was surprised by a statement he made. He noted that he frequented the local academic and public libraries and admired the librarians there, because they were such interesting people. Evidently, he had assumed that they were the exception to the rule. However he was surprised to discover during the week that most of the librarians he had encountered from all parts of the country were interesting people as well. On the flight back home, with that challenge to the stereotype still fresh in mind, David read an exciting article in an airline magazine that highlighted the significant role of librarians in the Information Age and today's high-tech environment.

Even more recently, the April 1994 issue of *Glamour* carried a stimulating article about how technology has transformed the work of librarians more than any other career. Describing librarians as information gurus, the article cited their use of cutting-edge technology. It drew responses from over 3,000 people who requested career information from the ALA Office for Library Personnel Resources.[20] Five months later the requests were still coming in. Some people who called commented that the article made them think of librarians in a new light.

The profession is filled with people who have stimulating, diverse, and well-balanced interests. It is hoped that this awareness will help librarians to consciously take pride in their profession and take responsibility for promoting it to others.

REFERENCES AND NOTES

1.Indra M. David, "Librarians Occupational Stereotype: Will it Ever Change?" in *Academic Libraries Achieving Excellence in Higher Education, Proceedings of the Sixth National Conference* (Chicago: Association of College & Research Libraries, 1992), 43.

2. Edward K. Strong, Jr., *Vocational Interests of Men and Women* (Stanford, CA: Stanford University Press, 1943).

3. John L. Holland, *Making Vocational Choices: A Theory of Careers* (Englewood Cliffs, NJ: Prentice Hall, 1973), 4.

4. Duane Brown, Linda Brooks and Associates, *Career Choice and Development; Applying Contemporary Theories to Practice*, 2d ed. (San Francisco: Jossey-Bass, 1990), 67.

5. John L. Holland, *Making Vocational Choices: A Theory of Vocational Personalities and Work Environments*, 2d ed. (New York: Prentice Hall, 1985), 7-11.

6. James V. Mitchell, Jr., ed. *The Ninth Mental Measurements Yearbook* (Lincoln, NE: Buros Institute of Mental Measurements, 1985), 1480.

7. Jo-Ida C. Hansen and David P. Campbell, *Manual for the Strong Interest Inventory: Form T325 of the Strong Vocational Interest Blank*, 4th ed. (Stanford, CA: Stanford University Press, 1985), vi, 48-49.

8. Jo-Ida C. Hansen, *User's Guide for the SVIB-SCII* (Stanford, CA: Stanford University Press, 1984), 26.

9. Hansen and Campbell, *Manual*, 77-86.

10. Hansen and Campbell, *Manual*, 28-29 and Hansen, *User's Guide*, 9-12.

11. David P. Campbell and Jo-Ida C. Hansen, *Manual for the Strong Campbell Interest Inventory*, 3d ed. (Stanford, CA: Stanford University Press, 1981), 62, 131.

12. Indra M. David, "Study of the Occupational Interests and Personality Types of Librarians" (Ph.D. diss., Wayne State University, 1990).

13. Pauline Wilson, *Stereotype and Status: Librarians in the United States* (Westport, Conn: Greenwood Press, 1982), 77.

14. Hansen, *User's Guide*, 10.

15. Gary D. Gottfredson and John L. Holland, *Dictionary of Holland Occupational Codes*, 2d ed. (Odessa, FL: Psychological Assessment Resources, 1989).

16. Hansen, *User's Guide*, 39.

17. Allen L. Hammer and Jean M. Kummerow, *Strong and MBTI® Career Development Guide*, (Palo Alto, CA:Consulting Psychologists Press, 1992), 57.

18. Allen L. Hammer, a telephone conversation with Mary Jane Scherdin, 27 January 1994.

19. "How Many Librarians Are There in the United States?" Fact Sheet No. 2 (Chicago: American Library Association, 1993).
20. Laurel Touby, "The New Librarian is an Info-Surfer," *Glamour* 92 (April 1994): 126. Margaret Myers, a telephone conversation with Mary Jane Scherdin, 24 August 1994.

Appendix
Descriptions of General Occupational Themes

Realistic (R): People manifesting the characteristics of this type are described as robust, rugged, and practical. They have good motor coordination and skills, usually perceive themselves as having mechanical ability, and like to build things with tools. They prefer concrete to abstract problems and avoid social settings that require verbal and interpersonal skills.

Investigative (I): People in this category include those with a strong scientific orientation. They usually are task-oriented, introspective, reserved, and not particularly interested in working around other people, preferring to think problems through rather than act them out. They enjoy ambiguous tasks, prefer to work independently and have unconventional values and attitudes. Regarding themselves as scholarly, analytical, and curious, they dislike repetitive tasks.

Artistic (A): Persons of this type prefer free, unstructured situations with maximum opportunity for self-expression. They resemble Investigative types in being introspective and preferring to work alone but differ in having a greater need for individual expression. They see themselves as original, intuitive, creative, nonconforming, and independent, and they value aesthetic qualities. They are less assertive about their own opinions and capabilities. Preferring to solve problems through self-expression, they avoid dealing with problems that are highly structured.

Social (S): This category includes those who are sociable, responsible, humanistic, and who like to work in groups and enjoy being at the center of the group. They have good verbal and interpersonal skills and prefer to avoid highly structured activities. Seeing themselves as understanding, idealistic, and helpful, they prefer to solve problems with feeling and through discussion with others. They enjoy activities that involve informing, training, developing, curing or enlightening others. They value social and ethical activities and problems.

Enterprising (E): People of this type have verbal skills suited to selling, are dynamic leaders, have a strong drive to attain organizational goals or economic aims, and tend to avoid work situations requiring long periods of intellectual effort. They have a high energy level and prefer social tasks where they can assume leadership. They see themselves as self-confident, enthusiastic, adventurous, and dominant.

Conventional (C): Conventional people prefer well-ordered activities, both verbal and numerical, that characterize office work and are effective at well-structured tasks. They avoid ambiguous situations and problems involving interpersonal relationships. They describe themselves as conscientious, efficient, obedient, calm, orderly and practical, and they value material possessions and status.

Vive la Différence: Exploring Librarian Personality Types Using the MBTI®

Mary Jane Scherdin

Introduction

Do librarians fit a distinct mold? What differences, if any, separate those who choose careers as librarians from those who choose other occupations? Are there differences among those who choose the library profession based on type of library or type of specialty within the field? These questions inspired the 1992 study on the vocational interests of librarians sponsored by the Association for College and Research Libraries (ACRL) reported here.

Recent career counseling literature has emphasized the importance of looking at the broader psychological and developmental needs of the individual.[1] Type theory and its measurement by the Myers-Briggs Type Indicator (MBTI®) has the potential to provide an approach to career choice that focuses on the whole person. It helps individuals to find tasks and problems that they will find interesting and challenging, and thus be rewarded for doing what they like to do and what they are good at doing. People who are matched with their occupations as well as with the organizations in which they work are more apt to be satisfied, to remain in their jobs, and to be productive employees.[2]

Swiss psychologist Carl Jung developed the theory of psychological types, and the MBTI® helps make this theory understandable and useful in people's lives.[3] Jung believed that human development is a lifelong process of striving toward completeness and that the growth process requires increasing self-awareness and self-acceptance.

Jung and Isabel Briggs Myers shared a fascination with individual differences and an optimism about human potential. Jung's premise was that all personality types are equally valuable, and each can make a special contribution. Myers believed that by making type knowledge accessible to individuals, she could help people achieve the kind of personal fulfillment that would benefit them as individuals and also contribute to societal progress.[4] Furthermore, the suffering and tragedies of World War II stirred in Myers the desire to do something that might help people understand each other and avoid destructive conflicts.[5]

Many individuals and groups have taken the MBTI® in order to gain insight into themselves and others, and to see differences as a source of interest and strength. With today's emphasis on teamwork, the MBTI® has become widely known and is frequently used as a management tool in the business world. For these reasons, the MBTI® was chosen for this study of librarians. According to Consulting Psychologists Press (CPP), publisher of the MBTI®, over two-and-one-half million people utilized the instrument in 1993. It is the most widely used and reliable personality inventory for exploring normal human behavior.[6]

MBTI® Preference Scales

The MBTI®, an inventory of preferences, indicates a person's innate predispositions on four dichotomous scales: Extraversion vs. Introversion, Sensing vs. Intuition, Thinking vs. Feeling, and Judging vs. Perceiving. The MBTI® definitions of these terms are atypical, and it is important to avoid misinterpretation.

The Extraversion/Introversion scale (E/I) describes whether a person focuses on and gains energy from the inner or the outer world. An Introvert's main interests are in the inner world of concepts and ideas, while the Extravert is more involved with the outer world of people and things. Extraverts are rated by others as outgoing, sociable, and talkative, while Introverts are described as quiet and reserved.[7]

Sensing (S) and Intuition (N) are two distinct ways of gathering information. When using the Sensing function, one becomes aware of things directly through the five senses, while Intuition is indirect perception by way of the unconscious, a sixth sense or "hunch". Sensing types are described as practical, conservative, dependable, precise, and methodical, while Intuitives are oriented toward the future, like to exercise creativity, tend towards independent rather than traditional views, and are inclined to see the overall picture.

Two ways of coming to conclusions or making decisions are Thinking (T), a logical, analytical approach aimed at objective decisions, and Feeling (F), judging subjectively and according to personal or social values. Thinkers believe it is more important to be right than to be liked, while persons with the feeling preference like harmony more than clarity. It has been said that Thinking types make decisions with their heads and Feeling types with their hearts.

The Judging/Perceiving scale (J/P) shows two attitudes for dealing with the outer world. Those with the Judging preference order their lives and are described as industrious and painstaking. They feel more comfortable when decisions are made and a schedule is in place. Those with the Perceiving preference are spontaneous, adaptable and prefer to collect information and stay open to new options. They are interested in starting new endeavors and like change. Further characteristics that describe each of the eight preferences can be found in Table 1. Contrasts are indicated across the columns from each other.

Table 1
Characteristics of MBTI® Preferences

DIRECTION OF FOCUS, SOURCE OF ENERGY	
Extraversion (E)	Introversion (I)
Outgoing, gregarious	Inwardly directed
Interaction	Quiet concentration
Breadth of interest	Depth of interest
Multiple relationships	Deep friendship
Active	Reflective
Speak, then think	Think, then speak
Energized by outer world	Energized by inner world
Focus on people, things	Focus on thoughts, ideas
WAYS OF TAKING IN INFORMATION	
Sensing (S)	Intuition (N)
Facts	Insights, possibilities
Sequential, step-by-step	Random, leap around
Present	Future
Reality	Fantasy
Practical, sensible, dependable	Ingenious, imaginative, visionary
Specific, precise	General, overall picture
Five Senses	Hunches, 6th sense
Patient with details	Patient with complex situations
Like to use established skills	Like to learn new skills
Dislike new problems	Like to solve new problems
WAYS OF COMING TO CONCLUSIONS	
Thinking (T)	Feeling (F)
Head	Heart
Objective	Subjective
Analysis	Sympathy
Impersonal	Personal
Critique	Appreciate
Reason, logic	Social values
Criteria	Circumstances
May hurt feelings unknowingly	Enjoy pleasing people
Justice	Mercy
Principles	Harmony
Firm but fair	Compassionate
Detached	Involved

ATTITUDES TOWARD EXTERNAL WORLD

Judging (J)	Perceiving (P)
Organized	Flexible
Planned, scheduled	Spontaneous, open-ended
Decisive, settled	Tentative, wait and see
Control one's life	Let life happen
Systematic	Open to change
Set goals	Gather information
Resolved	Pending
Structure, regulate	Flow

Just as one is born with a natural predisposition for right- or left-handedness but can develop skills if the other is needed, each person has the ability to use all eight of the above preferences. However, one preference on each of the four scales is more natural and feels more comfortable. These inborn preferences will be used more often and trusted more implicitly. The purpose of the MBTI® is to find a person's preference on each of the four scales and to combine them into a four-letter type, such as ENFP (Extraverted Intuitive Feeling Perceiving). There are sixteen possible types, each having unique gifts to offer. See Table 2 for a short description of each type.

The distinctions between people of different types are not merely a question of superficial tastes but are fundamental to their perceptions of the world. For example, Introverts work better in one-on-one situations rather than in large groups. Their energy comes from within, and they need time for reflection. In contrast, Extraverts draw energy from other people and do their thinking while they're talking. They "recharge" by being with people, while Introverts need time alone to rejuvenate.

In this chapter it is possible to give only highlights of Jung's complex theory of personality types. Please refer to the bibliography at the end of the chapter for further information.

1992 ACRL Study

As described in the first chapter of this section, the author distributed the Expanded Analysis Report (EAR) version of the MBTI® to a random sample of American Library Association (ALA) and Special Libraries Association (SLA) members in 1992. Unlike the commonly used 94-question form, the EAR is composed of 131 questions. Results of the EAR include scores on 20 subscales which add a depth of understanding regarding similarities and differences within types.[8]

Table 2
Descriptions of Sixteen MBTI® Types

SENSING TYPES — INTROVERTS

ISTJ Serious, quiet, earn success by concentration and thoroughness. Practical, orderly, matter-of-fact, logical, realistic, and dependable. See to it that everything is well organized. Take responsibility. Make up their own minds as to what should be accomplished and work toward it steadily, regardless of protests or distractions.	**ISFJ** Quiet, friendly, responsible, and conscientious. Work devotedly to meet their obligations. Lend stability to any project or group. Thorough, painstaking, accurate. Their interests are usually not technical. Can be patient with necessary details. Loyal, considerate, perceptive, concerned with how other people feel.
ISTP Cool onlookers—quiet, reserved, observing and analyzing life with detached curiosity and unexpected flashes of original humor. Usually interested in cause and effect, how and why mechanical things work, and in organizing facts using logical principles.	**ISFP** Retiring, quietly friendly, sensitive, kind, modest about their abilities. Shun disagreements, do not force their opinions or values on others. Usually do not care to lead but are often loyal followers. Often relaxed about getting things done, because they enjoy the present moment and do not want to spoil it by undue haste or exertion.

SENSING TYPES — EXTRAVERTS

ESTP Good at on-the-spot problem solving. Do not worry, enjoy whatever comes along. Tend to like mechanical things and sports, with friends on the side. Adaptable, tolerant, generally conservative in values. Dislike long explanations. Are best with real things that can be worked, handled, taken apart, or put together.	**ESFP** Outgoing, easygoing, accepting, friendly, enjoy everything and make things more fun for others by their enjoyment. Like sports and making things happen. Know what's going on and join in eagerly. Find remembering facts easier than mastering theories. Are best in situations that need sound common sense and practical ability with people as well as with things.
ESTJ Practical, realistic, matter-of-fact, with a natural head for business or mechanics. Not interested in subjects they see no use for, but can apply themselves when necessary. Like to organize and run activities. May make good administrators, especially if they remember to consider others' feelings and points of view.	**ESFJ** Warm-hearted, talkative, popular, conscientious, born cooperators, active committee members. Need harmony and may be good at creating it. Always doing something nice for someone. Work best with encouragement and praise. Main interest is in things that directly and visibly affect people's lives.

INTUITIVE TYPES — INTROVERTS

INFJ Succeed by perseverance, originality, and desire to do whatever is needed or wanted. Put their best efforts into their work. Quietly forceful, conscientious, concerned for others. Respected for their firm principles. Likely to be honored and followed for their clear convictions as to how best to serve the common good.	**INTJ** Usually have original minds and great drive for their own ideas and purposes. In fields that appeal to them, they have a fine power to organize a job and carry it through with or without help. Skeptical, critical, independent, determined, sometimes stubborn. Must learn to yield less important points in order to win the most important.
INFP Full of enthusiasms and loyalties, but seldom talk of these until they know you well. Care about learning, ideas, language, and independent projects of their own. Tend to undertake too much, then somehow get it done. Friendly, but often too absorbed in what they are doing to be sociable. Little concerned with possessions or physical surroundings.	**INTP** Quiet and reserved. Especially enjoy theoretical or scientific pursuits. Like solving problems with logic and analysis. Usually interested mainly in ideas, with little liking for parties or small talk. Tend to have sharply defined interests. Need careers where some strong interest can be used and useful.

INTUITIVE TYPES — EXTRAVERTS

ENFP Warmly enthusiastic, high-spirited, ingenious, imaginative. Able to do almost anything that interests them. Quick with a solution for any difficulty and ready to help anyone with a problem. Often rely on their ability to improvise instead of preparing in advance. Can usually find compelling reasons for whatever they want.	**ENTP** Quick, ingenious, good at many things. Stimulating company, alert and outspoken. May argue for fun on either side of a question. Resourceful in solving new and challenging problems, but may neglect routine assignments. Apt to turn to one new interest after another. Skillful in finding logical reasons for what they want.
ENFJ Responsive and responsible. Generally feel real concern for what others think or want, and try to handle things with due regard for the other person's feelings. Can present a proposal or lead a group discussion with ease and tact. Sociable, popular, sympathetic. Responsive to praise and criticism.	**ENTJ** Hearty, frank, decisive, leaders in activities. Usually good in anything that requires reasoning and intelligent talk, such as public speaking. Are usually well informed and enjoy adding to their fund of knowledge. May sometimes appear more positive and confident than their experience in an area warrants.

This chapter will summarize the results, including significant differences between librarians having various specialties within the field as well as those working in different types of libraries. Unless otherwise indicated, the sample group used for analysis was 1600 satisfied librarians with master's degrees in library science or library and information science who completed the Strong Interest Inventory, the demographic questionnaire, and the MBTI®.

Previous Librarian Sample

The Center for Applications of Psychological Type (CAPT) collects data on MBTI® research and has published the *Atlas of Type Tables* with reports on the frequency of MBTI® types found in various occupations. The information gathered between 1971 and 1984 from a limited sample of 267 librarians showed that the highest preferences were Introverted Sensing Feeling Judging.[9] The author's data from the ACRL study shows that the majority of librarians have Introversion, Intuition, Thinking, and Judging preferences. Comparing the two profiles results in highly significant differences on two of the four scales - Sensing/Intuition and Thinking/Feeling. Table 3 shows the data from the ACRL study compared to the earlier CAPT data.

Table 3
Comparison of Previous and Current Librarian Samples

PREFERENCES	CAPT SAMPLE *N*=267	ACRL STUDY *N*=1600
Extraversion(E)	39% E	37% E
Introversion (I)	61% I	63% I
Sensing(S)	54% S	41% S
Intuition (N)	46% N	59% N
Thinking (T)	33% T	69% T men 58% T women
Feeling (F)	67% F	31% F men 42% F women 61% T weighted average
Judging (J)	64% J	66% J
Perceiving (P)	36% P	34% P

A question that still lingers is whether librarians have changed or whether the initial information was not accurate because of sample size. CAPT prefers to have a random sample that is larger than 267; however, it was the only information that was available at the time the *Atlas of Type Tables* was published. The results of the current study have been forwarded to CAPT to be added to its Data Bank of occupations and will be published in the next edition of the *Atlas*.

Librarians and the General Population

A comparison of librarians with the general population as reported by Isabel Myers[10] reveals dramatic differences. Librarians are the opposite of the general population on Introversion (I) and Intuition (N), and women librarians are almost twice as likely as other women to have the Thinking (T) preference. A partial explanation for these differences lies in the fact that while Introverted Intuitive types are relatively infrequent in the general population, their numbers are more frequent at higher educational levels.[11] A preference for Intuition indicates a theoretical orientation that is associated with interest and comfort in college and university settings. Since librarians are among the most highly educated people in the population, their placement in this category seems appropriate.

Table 4
Comparison of Librarians and General Pupulation

PREFERENCES	ACRL STUDY OF LIBRARIANS	GENERAL POPULATION
Extraversion (E)	37% E	65% E
Introversion (I)	63% I	35% I
Sensing (S)	41% S	68% S
Intuition (N)	59% N	32% N
Thinking (T)	69% men T	61% men T
	58% women T	32% women T
Feeling (F)	31% men F	39% men F
	42% women F	68% women F
Judging (J)	66% J	55% J
Perceiving (P)	34% P	45% P

The data in Table 4 shows that library and information professionals are distinctly different from the general population. Significant differences were found on 14 of the 16 types. Only ISFJ and ENTP do not have significant differences. Twelve of the fourteen are highly significant (.001 level). See Table 5 for a visual comparison of the general population vs. librarians.

Table 5
Comparison of Librarians to General Population

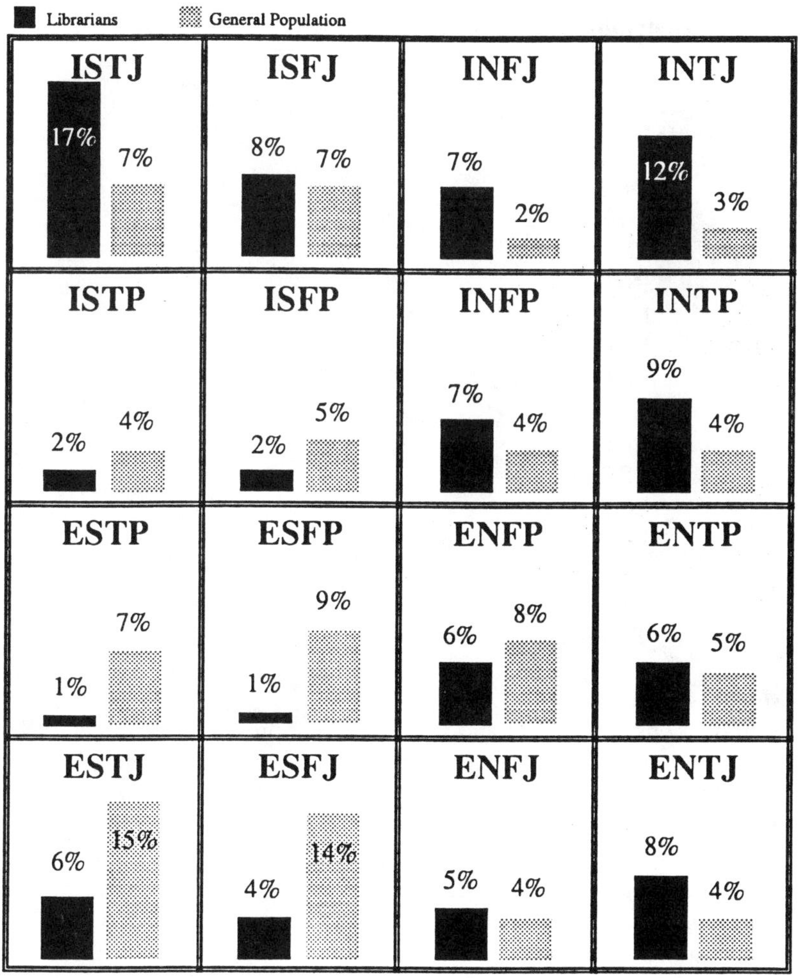

Tables 5 and 6 show that ISTJ (Introverted Sensing Thinking Judging) and INTJ (Introverted Intuitive Thinking Judging) are clearly the two types most often found in the ACRL study. While the majority of librarians are Introverted

(I), Intuitive (N), Thinking (T) and Judging (J), the greatest frequency for a given four-letter type is ISTJ. It follows that although there are more Intuitives in the sample, they are spread across several frequently found four-letter types, e.g., INTJ, INTP, ENTJ. Table 6 is a summary in rank order of the percentage of librarians in each of the 16 types.

Table 6
Distribution of Librarians in Each MBTI® Type

TYPE	FREQUENCY	PERCENT
ISTJ	265	16.5
INTJ	184	11.5
INTP	146	9.1
ISFJ	129	8.1
ENTJ	127	7.9
INFP	116	7.3
INFJ	104	6.5
ESTJ	98	6.1
ENFP	96	6.0
ENTP	94	5.9
ENFJ	81	5.1
ESFJ	66	4.1
ISTP	36	2.3
ISFP	27	1.7
ESTP	18	1.1
ESFP	13	.8
TOTAL	1600	100.0

Two Most Frequent Types
Brief introductions to the ISTJ and INTJ types are presented in Table 7. Since three of the four preferences are identical (Intuitive, Thinking and Judging), there are many similarities between the two types, such as being decisive, logical, productive, and reflective. The important difference is on the S/N scale. Interestingly, the S/N preference is thought to have the most influence on occupational choice in general.[12] Sensing (S) types are drawn to occupations that let them use their practical skills, where they can deal with facts. Intuitives (N) like situations in which they look at possibilities, think independently, and problem-solve at a systems level. This contrast, then, may influence the direction taken within the profession. Both Sensing and Intuitive types are needed in a library. The visionary Intuitive is needed to look at broad ramifications of problems and to generate ideas for fresh alternatives. The dependable, consistent, precise Sensing person makes others aware of pertinent facts.

Table 7
Brief Descriptions of ISTJ and INTJ

INTROVERTED SENSING WITH THINKING (ISTJ)

People with ISTJ preferences are extremely dependable and have a complete, realistic and practical respect for facts. They absorb, remember, and use any number of facts and are careful about their accuracy.

ISTJs are thorough, painstaking, systematic, hard-working, and careful with particulars and procedures. Their perseverance tends to stabilize everything with which they are connected. They do not enter into things impulsively, but once committed, they are very hard to distract or discourage.

ISTJs may overlook the long-range implications in favor of day-to-day operations. It is possible for them to become rigid in their ways and be thought of as inflexible.

INTROVERTED INTUITION WITH THINKING (INTJ)

People with INTJ preferences are relentless innovators in thought as well as action. They trust their intuitive insights into the true relationships and meanings of things. Problems only stimulate them—the impossible takes a little longer, but not much. They have determination, perseverance, and will drive others almost as hard as they drive themselves.

They are the most independent of all the types. They place a high value on competence—their own and that of others.

Although their preference is for intuition, they can, when necessary, focus on the details of a project to realize their vision.

INTJs may neglect their feeling values to the point of ignoring other people's values and feelings. Although their talent for analysis makes it difficult to show appreciation to others, it is important for them to do so.

ISTJs are quite dedicated to getting the job done, do so without fanfare, and pride themselves on being accountable. They may have trouble saying no and thus become overloaded. Since they are perfectionists, it may be difficult for them to delegate unless they have confidence in their subordinates.[13] They communicate a message of reliability and stability, which often makes them excellent supervisors. Since ISTJs are organized, thorough, factual, and careful in managing details, it seems likely that persons with this type would function well in structured tasks, such as those in technical services where consistency and accuracy are crucial.

In contrast, INTJs are confident, independent, ingenious, visionary, systems-minded, and like to plan and create. With their focus on efficiency, INTJs are single-minded in their work toward achieving a goal. They like to make things work, but when the task becomes routine, they prefer to move on to something else. They can develop strategies to solve complex problems or implement change, and they have an uncanny ability to project far into the future.[14] These qualities seem appropriate for managers and leaders as they work to implement long-range visions.

INTJs and ISTJs are often found as managers in the business world. It was noted in an article in *Fortune* that INTJs make up only a small percentage of the population but a disproportionate number of chief executives. ISTJs are "sticklers for detail and rules" and often become accountants and financial executives.[15]

It is interesting to note that ISTJ and INTJ were also the most frequent types found in studies of computer professionals in 1982-84. When compared with librarians, there were slightly more Introverts (67%), slightly fewer Intuitives (54%), more Thinking types (81%), and exactly the same percentage of Judging types (66%). Of the 1,229 computer specialists who took the MBTI® at that time, 73% were male.[16]

Types not found often in the library profession are ESTP and ESFP. ESTPs are highly gifted negotiators, entrepreneurs, and salespersons. Warm, charming and witty, ESFPs are masters at entertaining, showmanship, and sales.[17] Both types value first-hand experience, like to take risks, and respond to the needs of the moment. They tend to take charge in a crisis, have a direct and assertive style, and seek immediate results. Although they are adaptable, easy-going, and tolerant, they are usually conservative, valuing custom and convention. They have a great capacity for enjoying life.

Specialties Within the Profession

The ACRL study verified that there were significant differences among the specialties within the library profession. (See Table 8.) Note that not every participant answered every question; thus total responses may not always equal 1600. Of the five specialties studied - technical services, adult public services, children's public services, administration, and automation - the adult public services group is closest to being representative of the entire sample.

Table 8
Comparison of Specialties to Total Group

TECHNICAL SERVICES (*N*=217)
More Introverts*, Sensing*, and Judging types
More ISTJ, ISFJ*

CHILDREN'S PUBLIC SERVICES (*N*=190)
More Feeling* types
More INFJ, INFP, ENFJ

ADMINISTRATION (*N*=611)
More Extroverts, Intuitive, Thinking*, Perceiving types
More ENFP, ENTP, ENTJ

AUTOMATION (*N*=83)
More Introverts and Thinking types
More INTP*

ADULT PUBLIC SERVICES (*N*=489)
No significant differences

* denotes significance at the .001 level

There were significantly more Extraverts among administrators than in the rest of the sample. However, despite this difference, more than half (57%) of the administrators are Introverted rather than Extraverted. In contrast, 75% of technical services librarians and 73% of automation librarians are Introverted.

There are a greater number of Sensing types among technical services librarians, while there are more Intuitives among administrators. Percentages of Intuitives in the two groups are 63% administrators and 47% technical services. Administrators would be able to make use of the insight and visionary qualities of Intuition. Those in technical services need the sensing qualities of precision and patience with detail.

Significant differences were found on the Thinking/Feeling scale, with more children's librarians having the Feeling preference (56%). Feeling types tend to be tuned into the mood or climate in the workplace and tend to make decisions compassionately based on personal or social values. They have a need for affiliation, a capacity for warmth, and a desire for harmony. Feeling types are attracted to working closely with people and are concerned with the human as opposed to the technical aspects of problems. In contrast, more administrators and automation librarians have the Thinking preference (67% and 66%, respectively). Thinking types rely on principles of cause and effect and tend to be more impersonal when making decisions. They are objective, analytical, and concerned with principles of justice and fairness.

A separate analysis based on percentage of time spent on daily activities showed that those who said they spent over 50% of their time on reference (*N*=277) were significantly higher on the Feeling scale. However, still less than half (45%) were Feeling types as opposed to 39% for the entire sample. Since they have a strong belief in the values involved with helping people, Feeling types would most likely be happier in public service work.

There is also a difference on the J/P scale. More administrators showed a preference for Perceiving, although that percentage is still only 37%. When people are using their Perceiving preference, they are spontaneous, curious, open to new events and changes, and they aim to miss nothing. Administrators with the Perceiving preference may postpone making decisions while they search for options.

In contrast, 73% of the technical services librarians have the Judging preference. When using this preference, people are concerned with seeking closure, planning and organizing activities. When analyzing the data by type of activity, it was found that those who spend more than 50% of their time on cataloging activities (*N*=87) were significantly higher on both Introversion (76%) and Judging (80%) than the rest of the sample. These two preferences would serve catalogers well, since they need to focus in and be systematic in making decisions within the parameters of cataloging rules.

Type of Library

Differences were also found when comparing participants by the type of library in which they worked. (See Table 9.) Special librarians, including those who work in profit and nonprofit organizations, had no significant differences from the sample group as a whole. This was also true for the group called "other," which includes librarians from state library agencies, the federal government (including armed forces), and network/bibliographic utilities.

Similar to the children's public services librarians described above, school library media specialists were significantly higher on the Feeling preference than the total sample (52% vs. 39%). In contrast, more academic librarians were Thinking types (64% vs. 61%). Academic librarians were also significantly higher on Perceiving than the entire sample (37% vs. 34%). (Since there were no significant differences between the two- and four- year academic institutions, they were grouped together for this analysis.)

Table 9
Comparison by Type of Library

SCHOOL (*N*=136) More Feeling types More ENFJ*	PUBLIC (*N*=479) More INFJ
ACADEMIC (*N*=637) More Thinking and Perceiving types More INTP	SPECIAL (*N*=202) No significant differences

OTHER *N*=131
No significant differences
* denotes significance at the .001 level

Groups I, II, and III

When comparing the three major parts of the sample, Group I (ALA officers and committee members), Group II (ALA members) and Group III (SLA members), there were highly significant differences between Groups I and II on three of the four scales. Group I (*N*=730) had a greater number with preferences for Extraversion, Intuition, and Thinking in contrast to Group II (*N*=615) which had a higher number with Introversion, Sensing, and Feeling preferences. Again, it should be noted that, despite Group I's difference on Extraversion, more than half of the members were Introverted rather than Extraverted. Group III (*N*=255) had no significant differences.

It would be quite natural, according to type theory, for more Extraverts to be found in Group I; these people, whose attention flows out to the objects and people of the environment, would enjoy the discussions and people contact involved with committee work in ALA. Also the officers or leaders of groups would tend to have Intuitive preferences, since they like to solve new problems, look at possibilities, and focus on the big picture.

Years of Experience

Two sets of analyses were performed based on years of experience in the field. Each involved dividing the group into three sub-groups:

1) 0-5 years, 6-10 years and 11+ years
2) 0-10 years, 11-20 years, and 21+ years

Table 10 displays the differences that were found. In both comparisons, those who have been in the field either 0-5 or 0-10 years have a higher percentage of Feeling types, while those who have been in the field the longest periods of time have a significantly higher percentage of Thinking types.

Table 10
Differences by Years of Experience

0-5 years (*N*=172) More Feeling (47%) More INFJ	**6-10 years** (*N*=239) No significant differences	**11-47 years** (*N*=1,183) MoreThinking (62%)
0-10 years (*N*=411) More Feeling (44%) More ENFP	**11-20 years** (*N*=729) More ENTP	**21-47 years** (*N*=454) More Thinking (65%) More ESTP, ENTJ

A study of students at the University of Wisconsin-Madison School of Library and Information Studies (SLIS) verified the trend toward the presence of more Feeling types in the earlier stages of the profession. The MBTI® was administered by the author to students in the School's required management course in July and December, 1992 and April, 1994. A total of 109 students completed the instrument. There were significantly more Feeling types in the SLIS classes than in the ACRL sample. No significant differences were found between these students and those who had worked in the field 0-5 years on any of the four scales.

It is interesting to speculate about why there are more Feeling types in the group of librarians who are new to the profession. Is there a trend toward more Feeling types entering the field? Or do those with the Feeling function leave the field after a few years? Are they uncomfortable if an environment is strongly Thinking, where the atmosphere is objective and analytical, sometimes critical and impersonal?

A more likely explanation is that in the past, women who were Thinking types did not have a lot of career options open to them. (In the early 1900's, one library school had an exhibit that was entitled: "Careers for Women Other than Teaching".) Thinking type women may have felt that libraries were safe places for them to pursue intellectual interests in the days when it was not acceptable for females to show their intelligence. Now that more opportunities are available to women, the Thinking types may go into other careers, such as law, business, or higher education.

Reasons for Engaging in Occupation

Is MBTI® type related to a person's reasons for entering the library field? Participants in the study were given a choice of nine reasons for engaging in this occupation, from which they could choose as many as applied. Results in rank order were as follows:

Table 11
Reasons for Engaging in Occupation

REASON	NUMBER
I like to perform the activities it requires	1,395
I can use my best talents	1,202
I can make an important contribution	1,029
I can use my training	1,015
The working conditions are desirable	914
I can earn a good income	658
People tend to respect it	350
I fell into it by chance and have never left	262
I stand little risk of failure	92

Significant differences were found between some of these reasons based on MBTI® types. More Extraverts checked the following reasons: I can make an important contribution, People tend to respect it, I can earn a good income, and I can use my best talents. (Remember that a high percentage of the Extraverts are administrators.)

More Intuitives stated they could make an important contribution and that they could use their best talents. More Sensing types thought they could use their training, a natural tendency since they prefer to apply what they have already learned and work in familiar situations.

More Feeling types stated they could make an important contribution and that they could use their best talents. Values are important motivators for Feeling types. More Thinking types fell into the occupation by chance, rather surprising for those who make decisions so logically.

More Judging types are engaged in the occupation because they can earn a good income, while more Perceiving types said it was because they fell into it by chance, typical for Ps.

Table 12 shows a summary of the significant differences that were found for each of the 16 MBTI® types based on the following factors: gender, type of library, type of specialty, years of experience in the field, and reasons for engaging in the occupation.

Table 12
Summary of Differences

ISTJ Technical Services Catalogers	ISFJ Group II Technical Services Can use training Females	INFJ 0-5 years experience Group II Children's Public Services Catalogers Public Librarians	INTJ Males
ISTP	ISFP	INFP Children's Public Services	INTP Automation * Fell in by chance Males Academic Librarians
ESTP 21-47 years experience	ESFP	ENFP 0-10 years experience Administrators Make an important contribution	ENTP 11-20 years experience Group I Administrators Little risk of failure Fell in by chance
ESTJ	ESFJ Can use best talents Females	ENFJ Children's Public Services School Librarians*	ENTJ 21-47 years experience Group I Administrators Make an important contribution People respect it Can earn a good income Can use best talents

*denotes significance at the .001 level

Dissatisfaction
One question asked on the demographic questionnaire was, "How do you feel about your work?" with the opportunity to choose between four answers: "I am very satisfied, I am somewhat satisfied, I am somewhat dissatisfied, I am very dissatisfied." When analyzing those who chose the dissatisfied responses (*N*=125), it was found that there was a small but significant difference between those with Sensing and Intuition preferences. More Intuitives were dissatisfied (8% vs. 6%). One explanation might be that Intuitives, who would naturally be creative and far-sighted, might be frustrated by having to move slowly toward their goals. This would be particularly true for Judging types, found often in the library field, who want to make a decision and set an implementation schedule. Even though libraries have made dramatic technological changes in the last several years, they have been made in a very methodical and careful manner. In spite of the fact that there are a majority of Intuitives (59%) in the library profession, there are still a large minority (41%) who will want to make sure that each decision is analyzed carefully.

Expanded Analysis Report (EAR)
The EAR, a new version of the MBTI®, gives additional information than that found in the frequently-used Form G. It includes five subscales for each of the four MBTI® preference scales (E/I, S/N, etc.) See the Appendix for details of each subscale.

Scores on each subscale (0-10) reflect how much or how little an individual favors a particular trait. The closer the score is to zero, the more related the score is to the trait on the left, e.g., Gregarious. Conversely, the closer the score is to 10, the more related the score is to the trait on the right, e.g., Intimate. The traits on the left relate to Extraversion, Sensing, Thinking, and Judging. Parallelling these, the traits on the right relate to Introversion, Intuition, Feeling, and Perceiving.

Following is an example of one subscale on the Extraversion/Introversion scale:

Gregarious __1 __2 __3 __4 __5 __6 __7 __8 __9 __10 Intimate
*

The score of 8 indicates the person is more Intimate than Gregarious.

Average scores for librarians fell on the Introverted, Intuitive, and Judging sides of the scales (Table 13) thus confirming the highest preferences for librarians described earlier in this chapter. There was almost an even division on the Thinking and Feeling traits, with scores on Accepting and Tender falling on the Feeling side and scores on Questioning and Reasonable falling on the Thinking side. On the remaining subscale in the Thinking/Feeling area, librarians fell almost exactly in the middle (4.99) on Logical/Affective. According to the EAR guide, "middle scorers are more similar to those who are Affective people than to those scoring at the Logical end of the dimension. Those who are middle-scorers may experience tension over decision making since they want to consider logical consequences, but they can't put aside their concern for others' feelings."[18]

Table 13
Mean Scores on the EAR Subscales

TWENTY SUBSCALES	MEAN SCORE	PREFERRED TRAIT
EXTRAVERSION/INTROVERSION		
Gregarious/Intimate	5.49	Intimate
Enthusiastic/Quiet	5.82	Quiet
Initiators/Receptors	5.46	Receptors
Expressive/Contained	5.22	Contained
Auditory/Visual	6.08	Visual
SENSING/INTUITION		
Concrete/Abstract	5.99	Abstract
Realistic/Imaginative	6.54	Imaginative
Pragmatic/Intellectual	7.02	Intellectual
Experiential/Theoretical	6.22	Theoretical
Traditional/Original	6.28	Original
THINKING/FEELING		
Critical/Accepting	7.73	Accepting
Tough/Tender	6.92	Tender
Questioning/Accommodating	3.83	Questioning
Logical/Affective	4.99	Logical
Reasonable/Compassionate	4.37	Reasonable
JUDGING/PERCEIVING		
Stress Avoiders/Polyactive	4.33	Stress Avoider
Systematic/Casual	4.38	Systematic
Scheduled/Spontaneous	3.65	Scheduled
Planful/Open-ended	3.09	Planful
Methodical/Emergent	3.64	Methodical

Only one significant difference was found between librarians in various types of libraries on the EAR. School librarians were greater (6.54) on the Enthusiastic vs. Quiet trait than academic or public librarians (5.61 and 5.71, respectively).

The most differentiated scores (scores furthest from the middle) were for Accepting, Intellectual, Planful, Tender, and Imaginative, in that order. In other words, these are traits most often found in librarians.

Since the Accepting and Tender scores were outside of the expected pattern for librarians, i.e., toward the Feeling rather than the Thinking side of the scale, it may be useful to explore what the implications are. People who have the Thinking preference, but who score high on the Accepting subscale, appear to accept all ideas equally. They appreciate theories that challenge accepted knowledge. Their modesty about their own work, however, seems to inhibit them from promoting their own ideas with others. Their open and fair approach causes them to present all approaches as equally valid, respecting others' ability to choose among them.

People who are Thinking types, but who score high on Tender, do not see toughness as either an acceptable or desirable means of getting their way. They are concerned with how people feel about things and would rather depend on gentle persuasion and warm understanding to influence others.[19]

The traits that were found seem appropriate and desirable for librarians. In the public services arena, who could ask for a more suitable person to serve his/her information needs than an imaginative, questioning, intellectual who is accepting and tender toward the inquirer? Likewise, who could ask for a more ideal person for the behind-the-scenes, organizational work than a methodical, planful, and systematic individual?

Stress and Coping Resources

After looking at librarians' personality types, one may wonder how they meet and manage stress in their lives. Recent research by Allen Hammer of Consulting Psychologists Press tested the coping skills of the 16 types.[20] He confirmed previous findings that Introverts score lower on coping resources than do Extraverts. One explanation is that Introverts have fewer social supports due to less interaction with others. Self-esteem and optimism may be lower because they fail to test negative self-thoughts. The existence of a network of friends or a few confidants has been consistently shown to be one of the best predictors of coping.

In Hammer's study, in addition to the variance explained by the sixteen MBTI® types, the 20 EAR subscales predicted 41% of the variance on coping resources. The five EAR subscales that best predicted coping resources were Initiator/Receptor, Expressive/Contained, Realistic/Imaginative, Critical/Accepting, and Systematic/Casual. The poles of the scale most related to higher coping resources were Initiator, Expressive, Realistic, Accepting, and Systematic. Librarians on the average scored lower on Initiator, Expressive, and Realistic but higher on Accepting and Systematic.[21]

As stated above, the Initiator and Expressive traits help people to build support systems. Realistic people are efficient and practical, while those who are Imaginative seek constant change and novel situations, almost a definition of stress. On the other hand, Accepting people focus on the positive and the good, an attitude that is highly predictive of successful dealing with stress. Systematic people seem to be prepared for stress; they make plans in order to avoid surprises.[22]

When ranking the sixteen types by coping resources, as expected, all Introverted types ranked in the lower portion of the list. ISTJ and INTJ, the two most frequent types for librarians, ranked 10th and 12th, respectively. However, as noted above, even though most librarians were Thinking types, they scored as Accepting on the Thinking/Feeling subscale of the EAR - a plus for coping resources and one that might help them to move up in the ranking.

Librarians also scored near the middle on the Logical/Affective subscale, and, as mentioned above, middle scorers are more similar to those who are Affective people. "Affective people know what feels right, a resource that would serve to guide them through stressful experiences; stressors may not always yield to the logical approach of those at the other end of this scale."[23] Again, this trait gives librarians a plus for coping resources. In addition, the tendency to be Systematic may help balance the Imaginative tendency. In sum, librarians may have better coping resources than expected.

Recruitment Implications

The two most common types found in libraries, ISTJs and INTJs explore careers in similar ways. They prefer to have an action plan to meet their goals. They may have trouble utilizing unexpected opportunities and may be upset by unscheduled events. When making contact with people in the profession, they may not want to network but will logically see the need to do so and will contact carefully selected experts. They may appear too quiet in an interview, hesitating to "sell" their own strong points. It is possible for them to appear overly task-oriented or impersonal to potential colleagues. When making decisions about careers, they will conduct a logical analysis of alternatives, weighing the pros and cons of each; however, they must be careful not to make hasty decisions.[24]

There are some differences between ISTJs and INTJs in the career search process. When gathering information, ISTJs prefer to consult career libraries or databases for job-related facts and statistics, and they collect just enough facts to make a decision. INTJs will read about career opportunities or future trends and search for opportunities for growth and learning. In interviews, INTJs may focus on their potential and their ability to learn quickly, while ISTJs may present a detailed picture of their experiences in specific areas.[25]

Other Studies

It is possible that the sample used in the ACRL study could have been biased by the fact that it was made up of members of national library associations. In addition, it contained a small percentage of school librarians and a large percentage of administrators. In order to corroborate the findings of the ACRL study, comparisons were made to other recent studies that used the MBTI® with librarians.

School librarians in the ACRL study were compared to a small sample of media specialists ($N=106$) in the CAPT Data Bank of occupations. There were significantly more Intuitive Judging types in the ACRL study and more Sensing Perceiving types in the CAPT Data Bank sample which was gathered between the years 1971-1984.[26]

John Tyson studied 70 Virginia academic library directors in 1987 as part of his doctoral dissertation.[27] When compared with administrators in the ACRL study, three of the four most common types were identical: ISTJ, INTJ, and ENTJ. Similar to the ACRL study, the Tyson research also found that there were more Extraverts among library administrators. When comparing the academic library administrators in the ACRL study with Tyson's sample, there was one significant difference: Tyson's group had significantly more Judging types.

Carrie Coolbaugh's doctoral research in 1992 was based on a study of 69 California public library directors.[28] There were no significant differences between her sample and public library administrators in the ACRL sample. Most frequent types in the Coolbaugh study were ISTJ, ENTJ, INTJ and ESTJ.

In 1990, Special Libraries Association collected data from its members using the MBTI.® No significant differences were found when comparing the 1,413 SLA members with the 202 special librarians in the ACRL study.[29] As in the above studies, SLA's data also showed the most frequent types were ISTJ and INTJ. A summary of SLA results, 65% Introvert, 57% Intuitive, 65% Thinking, and 68% Judging, is remarkably close to the ACRL outcomes for all participants.

A study of Minnesota Library Association members from all types of libraries was conducted in 1986.[30] The MBTI® was mailed to 263 members and responses received from 226, 81% of whom were female. Results showed 59% Introvert, 66% Intuitive, 56% Thinking, and 70% Judging.

Comparisons of the earlier CAPT profiles for librarians and library support staff show a great amount of similarity between the two. (See Table 3 for CAPT data on librarians.) Both had Sensing, Feeling, and Judging preferences. Support staff were evenly divided between Introvert and Extravert. Unfortunately, the CAPT sample for support staff was quite small (N=84).[31] The author collected data from 68 Wisconsin library support staff at an MBTI® workshop in May, 1994, and this data resulted in the I, S, F, and J preferences for the majority of participants. If it is true that the profession is changing and that support staff have taken over some of the routine tasks formerly performed by librarians, it follows that the librarian profile would now be different from the earlier CAPT librarian profile and the support staff profiles.

The chapter in this volume entitled "Working Together" describes an extensive study of Texas librarians and support staff. Similarities and contrasts between the work in Texas and the ACRL study are explored in that chapter.

Conclusion

The fact that 63% of librarians have Introverted preferences has importance for the profession. While Extraverts show their first or best function to the outside world, Introverts save their best function for the inner world of ideas. Although a well-developed Introvert can deal ably with the Extraverted world when necessary, he/she works best, most easily, and most enjoyably with the reflective world of ideas. It follows, therefore, that Introverts are more likely to be underestimated in casual contacts.

In addition, Introverts are not as apt to initiate contact with others or to promote themselves. While Introverted public services librarians may have no problem approaching a patron to offer help, they may hesitate to originate contact with others either within or outside of the organization they serve, e.g., faculty in an academic institution. Most Introverts prefer personal, one-on-one interactions. Medium to large size groups, such as book discussions, are not as comfortable. Considering that the majority of the population is Extraverted, it may be easy for the general public to think of librarians as timid, lacking vigor, initiative, and self-confidence, since they are less comfortable with marketing themselves. Using the academic library example, librarians could take the opportunity to meet and greet as many faculty as possible on an individual basis and make a conscious effort to become involved in campus activities, such as working on small committees. Since Introverts need time to reflect before speaking, it is helpful to them to study the agenda prior to a meeting.

The profession is also affected by the fact that 66% of librarians have the Judging preference. Those with the Perceiving preferences need to be welcomed for the flexibility they bring to their work. Their curiosity and ability to see opportunities for change can be valuable assets to a library staff.

The survival of the library profession depends on diversity. As computers take over more of the custodial tasks of the library world, librarians are able to spend more time taking a leadership role in conceiving and creating ways to meet the information needs of tomorrow. They need to be capable of critical judgment in discerning patterns of future change.

The profession needs those who are accurate and good with detail (Sensing) as well as those with a holistic approach (Intuitive), those who get things done on schedule (Judging) and those who are open to new possibilities (Perceiving), those who plunge quickly into new opportunities (Extravert) and those with a more cautious approach but follow projects over a long period of time (Introvert), those who make an impersonal analysis of cause and effect (Thinking) as well as those who take into consideration how people are affected by plans and decisions (Feeling).

Knowledge of MBTI® types can be useful to help direct librarians to a good job "match" where they will be able to exercise their preferences and be happy in their work. As mentioned above, it is believed that the Sensing/Intuition and Thinking/Feeling preferences exert more influence over which occupation is chosen, while Extraversion/Introversion and Judging/Perceiving affect the kind of working environment chosen, once a field has been selected. Thus, if a librarian likes the academic setting but is unhappy in a large university library, he/she might be very happy in a small college setting.

In addition, if librarians are aware of the various types and how to work with them, they can help each other with problem-solving. People may be uncomfortable working with those with different preferences, but the differences often are essential for a good balance. "Comfort comes from being with people similar to us; growth comes from the differences of an alternative approach."[32]

If a librarian finds him/herself in a circumstance where his/her type is under-represented, e.g., an Extravert in a group of Introverts, he/she needs to find or create a special role within the situation, such as offering to lead book discussions, teach classes in the library, or represent the library to an outside agency. He/she might also seek out other Extraverts on the staff, or seek out Introverts who have two other preferences similar to his/her own.

We need to create a climate where our differences are seen as interesting and valuable rather than problematic.[33] Tasks that call on our strengths and preferences require less effort for better performance and give more satisfaction. Let's celebrate "la différence" that keeps us both satisfied with our profession and contributing to a diverse and complementary environment.

REFERENCES AND NOTES

1. Allen L. Hammer and Gerald P. Macdaid, *MBTI® Career Report Manual* (Palo Alto, CA: Consulting Psychologists Press, 1992), 2.
2. Allen L. Hammer and Jean M. Kummerow, *Strong and MBTI® Career Development Guide* (Palo Alto, CA: Consulting Psychologists Press, 1992), 5.
3. Isabel Briggs Myers and Mary H. McCaulley, *Manual: A Guide to the Development and Use of the Myers-Briggs Type Indicator* (Palo Alto, CA: Consulting Psychologists Press, 1985), 1.
4. Jean Kummerow and Naomi Quenk, *Interpretive Guide for the MBTI®Expanded Analysis Report* (Palo Alto, CA: Consulting Psychologists Press, 1992), ix.
5. Myers and McCaulley, *Manual*, x.
6. James V. Mitchell, Jr., *The Ninth Mental Measurements Yearbook* (Lincoln, NE: The Buros Institute of Mental Measurements, 1985), 1030.
7. Hammer and Kummerow, *MBTI,®* 32.
8. Kummerow and Quenk, *Interpretive Guide*, 1.
9. Gerald P. Macdaid, Mary H. McCaulley, and Richard I. Kainz *Atlas of Type Tables* (Gainesville, FL: Center for Applications of Psychological Type, 1986), 100.
10. Myers and McCaulley, *Manual*, 50-51.
11. Myers and McCaulley, *Manual*, 45.
12. Hammer and Macdaid, *MBTI® Career*, 36.
13. Olaf Isachsen and Linda V. Berens, *Working Together: A Personality-Centered Approach to Management* (Coronado, CA: Neworld Management Press, 1988), 194-202.
14. Ibid, 241-251.
15. Thomas Moore, "Personality Tests are Back," *Fortune* 115 (March 30, 1987): 74-82.
16. Macdaid, McCaulley, and Kainz, *Atlas*, 272.
17. Isachsen and Berens, *Working*, 121, 149.
18. Kummerow and Quenk, *Interpretive Guide*, 20.
19. Ibid, 34.
20. Allen L. Hammer, "Coping Resources and Scores on the Type Differentiation Indicator" (paper presented at the tenth conference of the Association for Psychological Type, Newport Beach, CA, July 1993), 7.
21. Ibid, 5.
22. Ibid, 6.
23. Ibid, 7.
24. Allen L. Hammer, *Introduction to Type and Careers* (Palo Alto, CA: Consulting Psychologists Press, 1993), 16, 28.

25. Ibid.
26. Macdaid, McCaulley, and Kainz *Atlas*, 102.
27. John C. Tyson, A Study of the Personality Type of Academic Library Directors in the Commonwealth of Virginia using the Myers-Briggs Type Indicator" (Ph.D. diss., Simmons College, 1988).
28. Carrie W. Coolbaugh, "Personality Types of Selected California Public Library Directors: Planning Implications" (Ph.D. diss., University of LaVerne (California), 1993).
29. Tobi A. Brimsek and Dolores Leach, "Special Librarians to the Core: Profiling with the MBTI®, " *Special Libraries* 81(Fall 1990): 330-37.
30. Bruce Willms, telephone conversation with author, 23 March 1993.
31. Macdaid, Mccaulley, and Kainz *Atlas*, 101.
32. Linda Rome, "Myers-Briggs: A Tool for Building Effective Work Teams," *Wilson Library Bulletin* 64 (May 1990): 42.
33. Myers, *Manual*, 5.

Select Bibliography

Hirsh, Sandra and Jean Kummerow, *LIFETypes*. New York: Warner, 1989.

Isachsen, Olaf and Linda V. Berens. *Working Together: A Personality-Centered Approach to Management.* Coronado, CA: Neworld Management Press, 1988).

Kroeger, Otto and Janet M. Thuesen. *Type Talk: The 16 Personality Types that Determine How We Live, Love and Work.* New York: Delacorte/Dell, 1988.

Myers, Isabel Briggs. *Gifts Differing.* Palo Alto, CA: Consulting Psychologists Press, 1980.

Myers, Isabel Briggs and Mary H. McCaulley. *Manual: A Guide to the Development and Use of the Myers-Briggs Type Indicator.* Palo Alto, CA: Consulting Psychologists Press, 1985.

Webb, Barbara. "Type-Casting: Life with Myers-Briggs." *Library Journal* 115 (June 15, 1990): 32-37.

Appendix
MBTI® Expanded Analysis Report

EXTRAVERSION VERSUS INTROVERSION

Gregarious: derive satisfaction from being with other people; join groups primarily to satisfy a desire for belonging and pursue popularity as a means to this end; generally poised; as much at home with acquaintances as with friends.

Intimate: derive satisfaction from maintaining complicated, informal relationships with a few significant others; seek deep friendships and real one-to-one involvements, even at the expense of superficial popularity; treat others as individuals, expect to be treated the same way.

Enthusiastic: want to be where the action is, to keep up with the action everywhere else; enjoy being the center of attention; contribute wit and humor to a group; can be noisy and flirtatious, or zany, impulsive show-offs; they feel that if life isn't exciting, it's not really life.

Quiet: prefer calm and serenity--even silence; not attracted to the center of action; avoid drawing attention to themselves; tend to present themselves modestly and conservatively; most comfortable with others who do the same.

Initiators: committed to acting as social facilitator; assertively outgoing; perform social amenities with finesse; build bridges between other people and help them to know one another.

Receptors: display little social initiative, tend to be quiet and shy--perhaps even to the point of silence; find social amenities relatively unimportant, and thus leave them to others.

Expressive: readily show their feelings and make their interests obvious; feelings expressed are typically positive--cheerful, warm, and humorous; usually find it easy to confide in others, and describe themselves as easy to know.

Contained: inhibit expression of their feelings and interests; describe themselves as difficult to know; their primary emotional responses are internal; may be difficult for them to confide in others, because the more upset they become the less they allow it to show.

Auditory: use sound as their preferred medium of communication; like to speak and listen, rather than to read and write.

Visual: like to read and write, rather than to speak and listen.

SENSING VERSUS INTUITION

Concrete: need to achieve clarity in perception; depend on facts, which they treat in a methodical, literal way; cautious not to go beyond the facts.

Realistic: prefer easy practicality and cost-effectiveness; pride themselves on common sense; place a high value on personal comfort and family security.

Pragmatic: maintain primary focus on material things; interested in physical comforts that can be experienced in the here and now; applications of an idea appeal more to them than the idea itself.

Experiential: rely primarily on direct experience; particularly cautious not to overgeneralize; may be fussy and adamant about details,, even at the expense of larger considerations.

Traditional: identify strongly with the familiar; admire and support established institutions or methods simply because they exist and provide a precedent.

Abstract: comfortable with the nonliteral interpretation of stimuli; more interested in the association value of a stimulus than in the stimulus itself, tend to be reflective and artistic.

Imaginative: enjoy the exercise of cleverness and ingenuity for their own sake; resourceful in dealing with new and unusual experiences.

Intellectual: maintain primary focus on mental virtuosity; tend to score well on IQ tests; enjoy the role of scholar and exercising their skills to acquire knowledge.

Theoretical: trust and use theory; just as happy inventing new theories as using old ones; spontaneously search for patterns in any array of facts; resourceful and insightful.

Original: strong sense of uniqueness; need to demonstrate originality; may be clever, inventive, and ingenious; adventurous and enterprising--take initiative to expound their original ideas.

THINKING VERSUS FEELING

Critical: argumentative and skeptical; take nothing for granted, concede nothing in return. May behave as if an adversarial state were normal, and view every situation as a potential "win-lose" opportunity.

Accepting: praiseful and forgiving; kind and tolerant toward others, they expect others to respond in the same way; view "win-win" resolutions of problems as possible and worth striving for.

Tough: use "muscle" to achieve objectives; one-sided quality to their toughness--relatively free of internal contradictions; frequently base interactions on the assumption that alternatives do not exist.

Tender: use affection and gentleness to achieve objectives; behind their tenderness lies an awareness that there are two mutually contradictory sides to many issues, making it impossible to reach purely rational resolutions.

Questioning: intellectually independent; like to think for themselves, even though some of their conclusions will not be automatically or widely shared by others.

Accommodating: manifest modesty and deference; like consensus and find that a simple way to achieve it is to agree with the viewpoints of others.

Logical: place heavy emphasis on the use of logic in everyday life; value and trust logic, their actual skill in employing it notwithstanding.

Affective: place heavy reliance on emotion in everyday decision making; value and trust their own feelings; whatever their effectiveness in using them.

Reasonable: demonstrably logical in everyday decision making; make effective use of sequential reasoning; confident and clear-thinking.

Compassionate: in touch with own emotions in everyday decision making; effectively know what they like and dislike.

JUDGING VERSUS PERCEIVING

Stress Avoiders: like to allow plenty of time so that an activity can be carried out efficiently, without fuss and bother; accomplish the most by doing one thing at a time, and seek to structure their lives in accordance with this rule.	Polyactive: find that a certain degree of stress facilitates any activity; happiest and most productive when trying to do several things at once; prone to let things pile up just to create a more satisfying challenge.
Systematic: interested in the thoroughness of the planning process, especially contingency planning; do not want to be caught by surprise; want to be prepared to deal with any situation.	Casual: high tolerance for surprise; comfortable taking things as they come and adjusting their activities as necessary; are typically described as leisurely.
Scheduled: comfortable with routine; regard tried methods and tested routines as the only reliable, efficient way to get things done; routine provides an important degree of comfort and security.	Spontaneous: uncomfortable with routine, which they view as a liability rather than as an asset; routine requirements likely to interfere with their responses to unexpected opportunities; usually have wide interests, so are typically exposed to many opportunities.
Planful: especially interested in long-range planning; regard it as their duty to be concerned about the future; focus energies and plan activities days and weeks in advance.	Open-ended: prefer to make decisions on the spur of the moment; value freedom, live in the here and now, like to "go with the flow," dislike being tied down by long range plans; want plans to be flexible.
Methodical: develop plans in great detail; program themselves in advance in a very thorough and precise way; identify and order specific steps well before undertaking any project.	Emergent: take an informal, ad hoc approach to problem solving; plunge ahead without detailed plans, even while recognizing the risks of such an approach--for example, that their actions may prove to have been hasty or careless.

Section III

Additional Information about Librarians and the MBTI®

Working Together: Research in Texas Libraries Using the Myers-Briggs Type Indicator

Nancy Boykin Bounds, Jennifer Patterson, and David T. Bailey

Do the Myers-Briggs types manifest themselves in job choices among Texas librarians and library staff? More specifically, is there a correlation between personality types and job classifications, such as administrators, public and technical services, professional librarians and support staff? Further, is there a correlation between personality types in libraries and gender, which is such a significant variable in library employment?

These questions emerged during a series of team building workshops sponsored by the Texas State Library and held throughout Texas. The Myers-Briggs Type Indicator (MBTI®) was administered at these workshops, and data have been analyzed to provide answers to the above questions.

During the workshops, librarians and support staff from all types of libraries discussed how improved understanding of MBTI® types might assist in staff communication and training, committee formation, institutional organization, problem solving, and planning. Through observation and discussion, there seemed to be a correlation between the roles an employee would want to play in a library and the individual's personality. There was very little published data, however, to test these ideas.[1]

Methods

Jennifer Patterson presented team building workshops to more than 40 libraries, consortia, or conferences in Texas during 1990 through 1993. The Self-Scorable Form G version of the Myers-Briggs Type Indicator was used.

Organizers of each workshop were encouraged to have all staff participate. For the most part the workshops represented a good cross section of library personnel, librarians as well as support staff, often including part-time pages and janitorial staff. In very few cases were the groups self-selected. Workshops were given at several conferences where people were voluntary participants; usually, however, the sessions were mandatory. As a state library consultant, Patterson worked primarily with public libraries, and the data are most extensive for that group.

The data collected during the workshops were supplemented by a letter sent to each site requesting additional information, including gender and type of position, for each of the participants. Ninety-two percent (92%) of the libraries responded, indicating a high interest in the project and subject matter. The Texas Library Association Directory was consulted for place of employment and position title for some participants.[2]

The resulting information was coded for MBTI® type, gender, type of library and position. Library types were academic, public, community college, school, special, state, and library school. Positions were divided by professional and support staff levels and by function. Librarians were further distinguished by administrative status. The definitions for these positions vary among libraries, thus all coding was done by one person who attempted to maintain consistency. The list, with operational definitions, follows:

Administrative librarians - includes library directors, district library coordinators, development officers, branch managers, and heads of areas, such as reference, circulation, interlibrary loan, AV, children's, special collections, technical services, cataloging, acquisitions, collection development, preservation, and systems;
Public services - includes reference, circulation, interlibrary loan, AV, children's and special collections;
Technical services - includes cataloging, acquisitions, collection development, preservation, and systems;
Support staff - includes public services, technical services, support services, and administrative office;
Other - includes pages, student workers, library board members, drivers, custodial staff, mail, and persons not employed in libraries;
Position unknown.

SPSS (Statistical Package for the Social Sciences), a comprehensive automated tool for managing, analyzing, and displaying data, was used to cross tabulate the variables and create percentages. Data were also run on the Selection Ratio Type Table, a software program written for the purpose of comparing type distributions. Tests of significance were run on variables using Chi-square and Fisher's exact probability.[3]

Results

Of the 1,336 participants, 82.5% were female and 17.5% were male. Of those whose classifications were coded, 36% were professional librarians, 45% were support staff, and 19% were placed in the "other" category.

Descriptions of the eight MBTI® preferences: Extraversion (E), Introversion (I), Sensing (S), Intuition (N), Thinking (T), Feeling (F), Judging (J), and Perceiving (P) can be found at the beginning of the chapter in this volume, "Vive La Différence."

Table 1 shows a comparison of the library employees in our sample to the United States general population. The main distinctions were in the Introverted and Thinking attributes. In Texas libraries, 59% were Introverts, which is roughly the reverse of that found in the population at large.

In the general population, a higher number of men typically score as Thinking types and women as Feeling types.[4] As expected, men in our sample were clustered in the Thinking types. What was surprising was that, with so many women in libraries, the Feeling attribute was not more evident. Fifty-one percent of females were Feeling types, about 17% lower than would be expected in the population as a whole.

In addition, differences were found on the Sensing/Intuition and Judging/Perceiving traits. More respondents were Intuitive and Judging than in the general population.

Table 1
Comparison of Preferences for
Texas Library Employees and General Population

PREFERENCES	GENERAL POPULATION[5]	TEXAS LIBRARIES
Extraversion/Introversion	65% E	59% I
Sensing/Intuition	68% S	57% S
Thinking/Feeling - Men	61% T	69% T
Thinking/Feeling - Women	68% F	51% F
Thinking/Feeling - (Weighted average)	52% F	52% T
Judging/Perceiving	55% J	63% J

Table 2 summarizes the rank order of personality types for the whole study and for the two main categories determined by professional status. Please refer to the chapter mentioned above, "Vive la Différence," for brief descriptions of each of the 16 types.

Table 2
Distribution of Myers-Briggs Types by Professional Status

TOTAL SAMPLE OF TEXAS LIBRARY EMPLOYEES *N*=1,336		TEXAS PROFESSIONAL LIBRARIANS *N*=480		TEXAS LIBRARY SUPPORT STAFF *N*=603	
ISTJ	16.5%	ISTJ	13.8%	ISTJ	16.6%
ISFJ	11.2	INFP	10.0	ISFJ	14.4
ESTJ	9.4	INTJ	9.6	ESTJ	10.6
INFP	7.6	ISFJ	7.9	ESFJ	7.6
INTJ	6.4	INTP	7.9	ISFP	5.8
ESFJ	6.4	ENTP	6.9	INFP	5.8
ENFP	5.7	ENTJ	6.5	ENFP	5.8
INTP	5.4	ESTJ	6.3	INFJ	5.0
ENFJ	4.7	ENFP	6.3	INTP	4.8
ENTJ	4.4	ENFJ	6.3	ESFP	4.5
ENTP	4.3	ESFJ	6.0	ISTP	3.6
ISFP	4.3	INFJ	3.8	ESTP	3.5
INFJ	4.3	ISTP	2.9	ENFJ	3.5
ESFP	3.5	ESFP	2.9	INTJ	3.5
ISTP	3.1	ISFP	2.3	ENTJ	2.7
ESTP	2.8	ESTP	.8	ENTP	2.3
	100.0%		100.0%		100.0%

Professional Librarians

Looking at the 480 professional librarians in the study, 80.5% were female. Percentages of participation by type of library were as follows: 45% in public libraries, 17% in academic libraries, and 17% in school libraries. Smaller groups included community college libraries, special libraries, and the Texas State Library. The vast majority worked in public services positions. About 36% held administrative positions.

As shown in Table 3, most Texas librarians were Introverted, Intuitive, Thinking, and Judging. These are also the most frequently found preferences in the national ACRL study of librarians presented in this book; however, significantly more Texas librarians were Feeling and Perceiving types. Texas librarians were slightly more evenly distributed through all preferences than the national sample of librarians. The ACRL study of librarians found significantly more INFJs and fewer ESFPs and INFPs than were found in this study of Texas librarians.

Table 3
Comparison of Preferences for Librarians and Support Staff.

	NATIONAL ACRL OF LIBRARIANS[6] N=1,600	TEXAS LIBRARIANS N=480	TEXAS STAFF N=603
Extraversion/Introversion	63% I	58% I	60% I
Sensing/Intuition	59% N	57% N	67% S
Thinking/Feeling - Men	69% T	71% T	66% T
Thinking/Feeling - Women	58% T	51% T	55% F
Thinking/Feeling - Weighted average	61% T	55% T	52% F
Judging/Perceiving	66% J	60% J	64% J

Looking back at Table 2, the most popular Myers-Briggs type for librarians was ISTJ (Introverted, Sensing, Thinking, Judging). ISTJs are analytical thinkers who are very productive, like facts and details, and work well independently.

The second largest group among professionals was the Introverted, Intuitive, Feeling, Perceivers (INFP). This level is about twice that found in the general population and significantly higher than the ACRL study of librarians. INFPs are very idealistic, and have high concern for social change and social justice.

The third highest incidence was Introverted, Intuitive, Thinking, Judging (INTJ) again higher than the population as a whole but not dissimilar to the overall population of college-educated people. This type thinks globally and is able to visualize systems and bring them into material reality.

There were few ESTPs or ISFPs. These are part of the SP group, poorly represented in libraries. Described as highly adaptable, they are troubleshooters, negotiators, action-oriented types.

As shown in Table 4, both sexes were highly ISTJ, but women were more evenly distributed among the types. Men had high numbers of INTJ, and women INFP. Men had the highest percentages with Introverted, Thinking, and Judging preferences; women had a higher percentage with Intuitive preferences.

Table 4
Distribution of Myers-Briggs Types by Sex

TEXAS LIBRARIANS				TEXAS SUPPORT STAFF			
Men		Women		Men		Women	
N=93		*N*=385		*N*=80		*N*=522	
ISTJ	19.4%	ISTJ	12.5%	ISTJ	16.3%	ISTJ	16.7%
INTJ	15.1	INFP	10.6	INTP	13.8	ISFJ	15.9
INTP	9.7	ISFJ	8.3	ESTJ	12.5	ESTJ	10.3
ENTJ	8.6	INTJ	8.3	INFJ	8.8	ESFJ	8.4
INFP	7.5	INTP	7.5	ENFP	7.5	INFP	6.3
ISFJ	6.5	ENFJ	7.0	INTJ	7.5	ISFP	5.9
ENTP	6.5	ENTP	7.0	ENTP	6.3	ENFP	5.6
ISTP	5.4	ESFJ	6.8	ISTP	5.0	ESFP	4.8
ESTJ	5.4	ESTJ	6.5	ISFJ	5.0	INFP	4.2
ENFP	5.4	ENFP	6.5	ISFP	5.0	ESTP	4.0
ESFJ	3.2	ENTJ	6.0	ENTJ	5.0	ENFJ	4.0
ESFP	2.2	INFJ	4.2	ESFP	2.5	ISTP	3.4
ENFJ	2.2	ESFP	3.1	ESFJ	2.5	INTP	3.4
ESTP	1.1	ISFP	2.6	INFP	2.5	INTJ	2.9
ISFP	1.1	ISTP	2.3	ESTP	0.0	ENTJ	2.3
INFJ	1.1	ESTP	.8	ENFJ	0.0	ENTP	1.7
	100.0%		100.0%		100.0%		100.0%

Administrative librarians were 78% female (compared to 82.5% in the entire sample) and predominately ISTJ and INTJ. The administrative category includes not only those who administer full-time but also librarians that work in other areas and have administrative duties. Significantly more administrators had Thinking preferences than non-administrative librarians. High levels of these types, along with ESTJ and ENTJ, would be expected among managers in the business world, but our results reflect a larger number of Introverts.[7] There were no ESTPs, and few were ISFP or ISTP, all in the SP group generally found less often among librarians.

Table 5
Comparison of Preferences for
Texas Librarians and Support Staff by Function

	ADMINI-STRATIVE LIBRARIANS *N*=169	PUBLIC SERVICES LIBRARIANS *N*=347	TECHNICAL SERVICES LIBRARIANS *N*=68	PUBLIC SERVICES STAFF *N*=263	TECHNICAL SERVICES STAFF *N*=156
E/I	57% I	56% I	75% I	60% I	59% I
S/N	56% N	55% N	52% N	67% S	71% S
T/F men	68% T	70% T	75% T	74% T	67% T
T/F women	59% T	52% F	65% T	54% F	54% F
T/F weighted average	60% T	51% T	68% T	50% T/F	51% F
J/P	63% J	61% J	60% J	63% J	63% J

Addressing distinctions between public and technical services librarians, it was found that in both cases, ISTJ (Introverted, Sensing, Thinking, Judging) predominated. Table 5 shows that technical services professionals were substantially more Introverted and possessed the Thinking trait much more often than their colleagues in public services. That the Extraverted Feeling types preferred public services was not surprising.

Of 76 professionals in school libraries, more were ISFJ and ISTJ. We had expected to find more ESFJs, a type which is very outgoing and people-oriented, and is often found among school teachers. The Sensing and Feeling traits were present significantly more often than for Texas librarians as a whole. Like the school librarians, the small number of community college librarians had a high percentage with Sensing preferences.

As shown in Table 6, community college librarians had the highest number of Introverts. Special librarians had the highest percentage of Extraverts and Judging types, while professionals in the state library had more with Intuitive and Perceiving preferences. Academic librarians exhibited the Thinking trait more often than their colleagues in other types of libraries.

Table 6
Comparison of Preferences for Texas Librarians and Support Staff by Library Type

PROFESSIONAL LIBRARIANS

	Academic Libraries *N*=79	Public Libraries *N*=207	Community Colleges *N*=39	State Library *N*=26	School Libraries *N*=76	Special Libraries *N*=35	All Types *N*=462
I/E	56% I	59% I	72% I	54% I	59% I	51% I	59% I
S/N	58% N	62% N	62% S	89% N	62% S	66% N	57% N
T/F	67% T	55% T	56% T	58% T	55% F	51% F	55% T
J/P	65% J	58% J	56% J	54% J	62% J	74% J	60% J

SUPPORT STAFF

	Academic Libraries *N*=150	Public Libraries *N*=316	Community Colleges *N*=54	State Library *N*=10	School Libraries *N*=31	Special Libraries *N*=40	All Types *N*=601
I/E	61% I	62% I	54% E	70% I	58% I	53% E	60% I
S/N	69% S	66% S	70% S	70% N	68% S	70% S	67% S
T/F	53% T	54% F	56% F	80% F	55% F	53% T	52% F
J/P	65% J	65% J	59% J	50% J/P	77% J	53% J	64% J

Support Staff
Among support staff participants, 87% were female, and 63% of those whose positions were known worked in public services. Public libraries were represented by 53% of the support staff in this study, with 25% in academic and only 5% in schools. Community colleges employed 9% of the group. Note that the "other" category is not included in the data analysis of support staff.

The majority of support staff in Texas were found to have the Introverted, Sensing, Feeling, and Judging preferences. (See Tables 2 and 3.) Support staff were more similar to the general population than to Texas librarians in the Sensing and Feeling traits, but more like librarians in Introversion and Judging. (Table 1) The most frequent type for both men and women was ISTJ; as shown in Table 4, the percentages were almost identical. The second highest type for men was INTP and women ISFJ.

Table 5 shows that public services and technical services support staff did not differ significantly on any of the four preference categories. However, tests of significance showed an unexpectedly large number of ESFPs in technical services, which seems unusual, since this type is very spontaneous and people-oriented.

Support staff in public libraries showed preferences for ISTJ and ISFJ. Those in academic libraries had a high number of ISTJs and ESTJs. Community college staff were often ESTJ, school library staff preferred ISTJ, and those in special libraries ISFJ.

Omitting the very small sample from the state library, public library staff were found to be the most Introverted group, and had the most Intuitives of the various library types. (See Table 6.) Support staff in community colleges had the most Extraverts and the most with Sensing and Feeling traits. More academic library staff were Thinking, while school library staff had more with the Judging preference, and those in special libraries exhibited the Perceiving trait most often.

Comparing librarians with support staff, there were differences in the Sensing/Intuition and Thinking/Feeling preferences. (See Table 3.) A higher percentage of professionals were Intuitive and Thinking. The Sensing/Intuition differences were highly significant. Ten of the sixteen personality types varied at significant levels for librarians and support staff. The greatest differences were that more librarians were INTJ and ENTP, while more support staff were ISFJ.

Functional Pairs

In discussing results, it is interesting to condense the sixteen Myers-Briggs cells into four preference groupings called functional pairs. The middle two traits, Sensing/Intuition and Thinking/Feeling, indicate how individuals gather information and make decisions. Using these two traits, the sixteen types become four groups, ST, SF, NF, and NT. Isabel Myers considered these "the most important factors by which to group the preferences."[8] They have been shown to influence work behaviors and are a useful and manageable way to study problem solving and career choice.

STs are more task-oriented than people-oriented, are not generally risk-takers, and can be counted upon for logical, rational, highly reasonable decision making.

SFs are often harmonizers. They support group goals and work toward cohesion, changing things by working the system from within.

NFs are likely to be impulsive and future-oriented. They tend to trust their intuition, may be less disciplined about time, and are conceptual thinkers. NTs are intellectual, pragmatic, and independent. They are often seen as controllers and take-charge people, and will focus on tactics that achieve specific results.

Table 7 compares three categories of Texas library employees by their functional groupings. It was found that most support staff in Texas were ST and SF. These Sensing types are very task-oriented and are able to process large amounts of information, but they may resist change. The sample of non-managerial librarians had more NTs and NFs. These are both Intuitive types, which are visionary and innovative. Texas administrators were more NT and ST. These Thinking types tend to be very logical and objective.

Table 7
Comparison of Functional Groupings for Texas Support Staff, Non-Managerial Librarians, and Administrative Librarians

Functional Pair	Support Staff *N*=603	Non-Managerial Librarians *N*=299	Administrative Librarians *N*=169
ST	34%	22%	27%
SF	32%	21%	18%
NF	20%	28%	22%
NT	13%	29%	34%

Table 8 illustrates how the functional pairs may approach the work place differently. It is a sample chart taken from one of the team building workshops. Small groups, divided by functional type, answered questions concerning their image of the ideal organization. This table illustrates some of the ways that one's view of the ideal organization varies along functional group lines and points out some of the similarities and differences that will be experienced in interaction among types.

Table 8
Sample Chart of Ideal Organization,
As Described in Team Building Workshops

	ST	SF	NF	NT
1. STRUCTURE How are tasks assigned?	By ability, experience, education, interest. Match skill to task.	By ability, interest. Who is best suited.	By interest, desire. Experience, knowledge, capability.	By capability, experience, interest, ability.
How is work sequenced?	By mission of organization, patron need, goals, priorities.	By deadlines, patron needs.	By team, long term goals in priority order.	By vision, priorities and resources. Logical, by objectives.
Who has control?	Supervisor, personal control. By team.	Good leader, group control with supervisor.	Team control with project manager. Complete autonomy, self management.	Me, with top leadership.
2. OPERATING MECHANISM What are the career paths?	Knowledge and productivity, expertise.	By merit, interest, and training.	Excellence, with occasional job shake-up.	Stable position with rewards for experience.
What is the compensation and reward system?	Recognition, salary, flexibility.	Verbal praise, responsibility, salary, flex-time.	Choice of financial, recognition, flex-time.	Money, recognition, flexible schedule.
How does information and communication flow?	Open, top down, bottom up. Lateral. Meetings, discussions, and written.	Free and informal, meetings and memos, written and spoken. Lateral.	All directions, open door policy. Lots on all levels.	Top down, bottom up, and lateral. Oral and written.
What should the rules and regulations be?	General and limited. Minimal, fair, flexible, structured, empowering.	Clear with flexibility. Strict but fair, open to change.	General rules, adapt to situation. Respectful, clear goals, few rules.	Goal oriented. Minimal, flexible, externally driven.
What are the ways that problems are resolved?	With management. One to one, supervisor arbitrates, group discussion.	Immediately resolved, chain of command. Consensus and group discussion.	Brainstorming, negotiating, consensus.	Solved at lowest level, consensus. Administration ultimately responsible.

	ST	SF	NF	NT
3. PEOPLE ENVIRONMENTS What kinds of people are preferred for subordinates, clients, peers, supervisors, customers, etc.	Co-workers: flexible, positive, cooperative, dependable. Clients: respectful, considerate, specific. Supervisors: open-minded, organized, encouraging, considerate.	Co-workers: hard-working, amiable, responsible, ethical. Clients: polite, cooperative. Supervisors: knowledgeable, organized, hard-working, goal oriented.	Co-workers: hard working, self-starters, creative. Clients: appreciative, intelligent. Supervisors: fair, respectful, hard working.	Co-workers: motivated, innovative, flexible, competent, tolerant, visionary. Clients: easy to work with, responsive, appreciative.
4. CLIMATE What degree of formality is desired?	Comfortable. Professional, flexible, task specific.	Friendly, professional.	Professional, but casual.	Respect. Mostly casual.
What kinds of clothing and offices are preferred?	Functional and appropriate clothing. Comfortable, private offices.	Appropriate clothing. Clean, open offices, with some privacy.	Clothing depends on situation, casual, neat. Offices reflect individual style, open.	Appropriate clothing. Offices professional, private. Both: practical, attractive.
What values does the organization serve?	Service, staff commitment. Integrity, intelligence.	Service, productive yet friendly.	Honesty, service.	Service, knowledge, integrity, liberty.
What are the organization's norms? What is it really like?	Honesty, consult widely. Friendly, service, productive.	Same as its people.	Honest, open, sincere.	Focused, tolerance, respect. Customer-oriented.

Comparison With ACRL Study

Significantly more Texas librarians had Feeling and Perceiving preferences than the ACRL sample of librarians. This could reflect a regional difference or might be explained by the methodological variations between the two studies. Sampling and administration of the MBTI® were handled differently. For instance, the ACRL study included an element which allowed it to select only librarians with the master's degree. Such a distinction was not included in this study. In addition, the ACRL sample was made up of three parts: members of the American Library Association (ALA), officers and committee members in ALA, and members of the Special Libraries Association (SLA). It is interesting to note that the Texas librarians showed more similarity to the ALA general membership, that is, the portion of the ACRL sample who were ALA members but not officers or committee members in ALA.

When comparing the two studies based on type of library and position, public services librarians in Texas had more with Extraverted and Perceiving preferences, technical services more with Perceiving preferences, school librarians more with Sensing traits, and public librarians more with Perceiving. There were no significant differences between the Texas academic and special librarians and their counterparts in the ACRL study.

Conclusion

This study found differences in personality types among most of the groups identified; thus workshop observations were supported by the data. Employees in Texas libraries varied considerably from the general population, with library employees being Introverted, Intuitive, Thinking and Judging.

Significantly more administrative librarians were Thinking types than other Texas library professionals. It may be that Feeling types are uncomfortable risking the potential loss of harmony common in administrative positions.

Librarians and their support staff had many differences in type. More librarians were Intuitive and Thinking, and more support staff Sensing and Feeling. In general, Intuitive types are more likely to pursue higher educational levels than Sensing types.

Public and technical services librarians varied in the Introverted and Thinking traits, but support staff in those service areas did not vary noticeably in personality types. There were also distinctions by gender, with more male librarians having Introverted and Thinking preferences than females. There were scattered differences exhibited in the various types of libraries, especially by professional status, but small sample sizes made generalizations unreliable.

Some issues arise from these findings. Although the public services area has more Extraverts and Feeling types, most librarians and support staff are clearly Introverted Thinking types. Introverted Thinkers would normally be less comfortable meeting the public, and the majority with these preferences do work in technical services; yet there are many who work in the public services area.

Although support staff, professionals, and administrators vary in personality, it is important that all strengths and preferences be combined to create an organization that works together and serves well. Our tendency is to hire people like us; being aware of the virtues of all types may help us reach beyond that.

Knowledge of personality type changes the interaction among co-workers, even if it is not built into the organizational chart or used in hiring. The authors have been told by professionals and staff in Texas libraries that the understanding of type preferences has brought changes in work groups and improved communication. People adapt in positive ways when they have a knowledge of type. While our research is only a beginning, it does show that the Myers-Briggs Type Indicator can offer theoretical and practical answers to libraries.

REFERENCES AND NOTES

1. Gerald P. Macdaid, Mary H. McCaulley, and Richard I. Kainz, *Atlas of Type Tables* (Gainesville, FL: Center for Applications of Psychological Type, 1986), 100-101.
2. Texas Library Association, *Directory of Members, 1992-1993* (Austin, TX: Texas Library Association, 1992).
3. J. Glenn Granade, Harold H. Hatfield, Steven S. Smith and Jacquelyn Beasley, *The Selection Ratio Type Table PC Program* (Gainesville, FL: Center for Applications of Psychological Type, 1987).
4. Otto Kroeger and Janet M. Thuesen, *Type Talk at Work* (New York, NY: Delacorte Press, 1992), 22.
5. Macdaid, McCaulley, and Kainz, *Atlas,* 41-43.
6. Mary Jane Scherdin, "Vive la Difference," in this volume.
7. Kroeger and Thuesen, *Type Talk ,* 394-396.
8. Sandra Krebs Hirsh and Jean M. Kummerow, *Introduction to Type in Organizations* (Palo Alto, CA: Consulting Psychologists Press, 1990), 11.

Select Bibliography

Brimsek, Toni, and Dolores Leach. "Special Librarians to the Core: Profiling with the MBTI®," *Special Libraries* 81 (Fall 1990): 330-337.

Hirsh, Sandra Krebs. *Using the Myers-Briggs Type Indicator in Organizations: a Resource Book.* Palo Alto, CA: Consulting Psychologists Press, 1985.

Myers, Isabel Briggs, and Peter B. Myers. *Gifts Differing.* Palo Alto, CA: Consulting Psychologists Press, 1980.

Webb, Barbara. "Type Casting: Life with Myers-Briggs," *Library Journal* 115 (June 15, 1990): 32-37.

Using the MBTI® for Team Building

Maureen Sullivan

I. Introduction

Teams increasingly are being recognized as the most effective way to accomplish work in libraries and information agencies. While many staff in these organizations have had experience in committees, task forces and work groups, most are just beginning to understand what a real team is and how teams can make a difference in both individual performance and overall organizational success. I have found the Myers-Briggs Type Indicator (MBTI®) to be an effective tool for helping work groups in a variety of settings to become teams.

A. How Does a Team Differ from a Group?

Real teams develop when a group of individuals (usually no fewer than five and no more than nine) learn to work together to accomplish results. In learning to work together effectively, the members of the team:

- develop a shared commitment to the purpose and goals of their assignment or task
- hold each other mutually accountable for the individual and collective results of their work
- identify individual capabilities, strengths, weaknesses, needs and interests; appreciate differences and deal with the conflict that inevitably arises when different points of view are expressed
- establish a structure for their work in which there is full participation, shared leadership, trust, support, open and direct communication, and an effective use of time and energy for solving problems and achieving the expected performance results

B. What Is Team Building?

Team building is a deliberate process through which a work group learns how to work effectively together. This is a process that takes time and requires the commitment and discipline of team members. It focuses on the interpersonal dynamics of the relationships among team members and requires a willingness to identify and remove blockages to team learning and development. Understanding what each member of the team brings to the team (strengths, weaknesses, needs, and interests) is critical to the team's ability to assess its capabilities and its needs for learning and development. Effective team building is an ongoing process that is directed at the needs of team members and requires management support and recognition.

There are several models that describe the key stages through which groups progress to become mature, effective teams. The one proposed by B.W. Tuckman and M.A. Jensen describes the developmental stages in short, descriptive terms that are easy to remember: forming, storming, norming and performing.[1] These four stages are sequential and developmental. A group must successfully work through the activities and resolve the critical issues of each stage before moving on to the next one. During each stage, group members will display a set of characteristic behaviors for that stage. To successfully move through a stage to the next one, group members will need to learn and practice a set of skills and abilities that will enable the group to move forward through the stages of its development. The stages and characteristic behaviors are summarized below:

Stage One: Forming In this initial stage, members are getting oriented to each other and the work of the group. They tend to be friendly, polite, interested and somewhat cautious toward each other. Some members may be uncertain about their roles and most are likely to be uncertain about what is expected of them. Learning about each other's skills, capabilities, behavioral style, and personal goals is important at this early stage.

Stage Two: Storming As members learn about each other, differences in style, ideas, and ways of approaching the work emerge. Conflict is a natural outcome of this exploration of differences. Members learn to acknowledge and deal openly with their differences. They listen attentively and actively to each other. In addressing differences they focus on the issues, not personalities; they search for alternatives; and they treat disagreement as a "group issue", not just the responsibility of the individuals involved. As the group learns to deal effectively with differences, they further clarify the overall purpose of the group, learn how to support each other, and begin to determine ways to solve problems as a group.

Stage Three: Norming At this stage the group comes together. Members are committed to the success of the group as a whole. They have learned to respect and accept each other and the differences among them. Individual contributions are acknowledged, feedback is given and received as the work proceeds, ideas and feelings are willingly shared in an atmosphere of trust and mutual support, and the group develops a strong commitment to achieving the results expected. The group establishes a structure for its work and agrees to engage in those behaviors that will facilitate its work.

Stage Four: Performing The team is highly productive. Team members are focused on task achievement and attend to interpersonal issues and needs as they arise. The team solves problems collaboratively with each member contributing as much as he or she can. There is a team identity and a high degree of trust among the members. The team is flexible, innovative and highly skilled at solving problems and making decisions. There is a high degree of energy and a strong commitment to achieving the best results in the team's work as well as for each member of the team. Team members are highly productive and genuinely enjoy their collaboration.

The time, energy and commitment necessary for team building raises questions about why organizations should invest in such an effort. Aa administrators and managers in libraries and information agencies strive to improve quality, meet expectations of users in today's complex information environment, and manage with reduced or status quo budgets, they find that many problems cannot be solved by one or two individuals and that an increasing number need to be addressed by the staff who are performing the work. In the past few years, a number of organizations, including libraries and information agencies, have established teams. In some, the team is becoming the key component in the organizational structure. Process improvement teams, self-directed work groups, self-managing work teams, project teams, cross-functional teams and quality improvement teams are being formed in a variety of library organizations.

C. Benefits of Teams

Some frequently cited benefits of teams are: faster and more flexible response to problems, meaningful employee involvement, improved work methods, better service, fewer levels of management, higher quality decisions, greater productivity, more efficient use of resources, and an increase in staff skills and motivation. These benefits are very important to the work environment in libraries today and will continue to be important to meet the challenges of the future.

II. The MBTI® as a Tool for Team Building

The MBTI® can make a significant difference in the development of a team. It helps individual team members to increase their awareness of their own behavioral style and preferences. It provides a framework for understanding the interpersonal interactions among team members and the resulting dynamics of the team. Individual differences in communication style, dealing with conflict, exercising influence and leadership, approaching problems, and making decisions can be discussed and fully explored within this framework. Team members are able to see individual and collective areas of strength as well as pinpoint any areas of weakness. This assessment of strengths and weaknesses can lead to identification of potential problem areas for the team and its work. It provides to individual team members and the group as a whole information that can effectively be used at each stage of the team's development.

The MBTI® is most effectively used in team building by a facilitator who is trained in the administration of MBTI®, knowledgeable about team building and group development, and experienced in working with groups, and who has a strong commitment to the success of the team. The facilitator must establish rapport and a climate of trust early in the relationship with the team.

A. Applications

I have used the MBTI® as a tool for team building in a variety of settings during the past seven years. The groups have included task forces, steering committees for strategic planning, several reference departments, the full staff in a departmental library, work teams in technical services operations, senior management groups, and, in one case, an emerging team-based organization. From this experience, I believe the administration of the MBTI® is an excellent way to begin the team building process. It helps most groups move through the early stages of their development more quickly and with a better understanding and appreciation of the contributions of individual members. It helps the group perform more effectively sooner. In at least one case, the MBTI® helped the group to complete its work well in advance of the target date for completion. I find it to be so beneficial that I suggest its use at the start of every project in which I have a role in helping a group or team in its development.

B. Work Groups

When the MBTI® is used with a group of staff in a department or work unit, it helps individuals not only to understand how they can work more effectively together in the future but to see why they have had successes and particular problems in the past. It provides an objective means for discussion of personal preferences and allows for more open discussion of what each person tends to do that helps or hinders the work of the department. In my experience, the initial conversation usually focuses on who shares what behavioral tendencies. There tends to be a lot of interest in how we are similar. The discussion then moves to the ways in which the MBTI® sheds light on interpersonal difficulties in the past and the ways in which we are different.

C. Management Teams

Of particular benefit to management teams is that the MBTI® helps to clarify leadership style preferences. In my experience the initial discussion of strengths and weaknesses, similarities and differences, and preferences among the group members paves the way for a closer examination of individual styles. Open discussion of such difficult and critical issues as beliefs about management and leadership, attitudes toward staff, varying ideas about organizational priorities, and personal preferences for solving problems and making decisions can lead to clarification of the management team's philosophy and to the development of a shared philosophy of management for the organization. In one library, members of the senior management team found it difficult to communicate problems to the Director. An examination of the differences in style led to a better understanding about why this communication was so hard and to an explicit agreement about when and how this information would be shared in the future.

D. Project Teams

Recently I have administered the MBTI® to several steering committees and task forces that have had specific responsibility for planning or problem solving on projects with relatively short time tables. In each case, the members of the group had known the other members, but they had not worked together before. The groups were expected to accomplish a major activity for the library at the same time that each member continued to meet the usual performance expectations of his or her work. Often such groups are eager to begin work on the task at hand. Usually there is limited understanding of the need to attend to the relationship issues in the group or to the need for the group to develop its ability to collaborate and perform as a team. The major benefit of the MBTI® to such groups is that it helps to reveal the strengths, weaknesses and preferences of each member and to uncover individual blind spots early in the group's experience. When this knowledge is available to the group, decisions about who does what can be made by matching the person to the task or activity, and agreements about work structure and procedures can be made with an understanding of individual preferences. The MBTI® also makes it easier for members to talk about how they interact with each other. This communication often leads to more effective use of meeting time and the identification of better ways to accomplish work. In the cases mentioned above, each of the projects were completed in nine months to a year.

E. Team-based Organizations

I had the opportunity and challenge of helping one library organization prepare its staff to work in a new organizational structure involving work teams. An early step in this transition to a team-based organization was a two-day team building workshop for the entire staff. Of course, scheduled time away and last minute emergencies prevented everyone from attending, but about 90% of the staff were able to participate.

Given the size of the group and the significance and magnitude of the organizational change they were experiencing, special advance planning was required. Several weeks before the workshop, I sent a memorandum to each staff member to introduce them to the MBTI®, to explain why I wanted them to complete it and to describe how I would use it in the team building session. Everyone was asked to complete the MBTI® but no one was forced to do so. A library staff member coordinated the distribution of the forms and booklets, and only a few members of the staff elected not to complete the form. I personally gave each staff member his or her results in the workshop. During the session, I provided the usual background information and explanation about the MBTI® and emphasized its potential value to the newly-formed teams. Follow-up sessions were held for those who could not attend the program.

As one might expect, the teams in this library have made varying uses of the MBTI® in their efforts to develop. Decisions about how and when to use the information rest with each team. Local resources are available to assist the teams in their work. The formal assessment of this organization's effectiveness in its reorganization will offer an important opportunity to evaluate the role of the MBTI®.

The MBTI® can be used in a variety of settings with different types of groups to facilitate development. Careful planning is required to assure acceptance of the results and optimum use of the information by the group. The following guidelines are offered to assist in the successful use of this important tool for group development.

F. Suggested Guidelines for Use of the MBTI® in Team Building

- Determine the reasons and purpose of the team building effort. Be sure it will be a worthwhile expenditure of resources, including the time of the participants.

- Clarify the roles and responsibilities of everyone who will be involved: the team leader, the facilitator, team members and administrators who may be sponsoring but not participating in the effort.

- Explain the MBTI®, how it was developed, how it is used, and the potential benefits to the team building process.

- Administer the MBTI® early in the group's development but not at the very first session. The information gleaned will be very helpful in the early stage but it will be helpful for members to have had some experience with each other before the MBTI® is introduced.

- Do not force anyone to complete the MBTI®. Completion should be voluntary and based on willingness and interest in learning from the results.

- Observe confidentiality. The decision to share the information about the results should be the prerogative of each person on the group or team. I usually develop a group or team profile but I do not divulge the names of the individuals associated with each type without their permission. An important step in the process of using the MBTI® for team development is when members tell each other their results.

- Hold the initial discussion of the MBTI® results in a comfortable, private place that is free from interruptions. Allow sufficient time (two to three hours) for the explanation of basic MBTI® information, dissemination of results, discussion of implications for the team's development and its work, and for identification of what individuals and the group as a whole can do to use the information to enhance team and individual development.

- Allow individuals to interpret and understand their own results before they are called upon to share them with others. Individuals should have the opportunity to validate the results with what they already know about themselves from their own experience.

- Prepare and post a group profile. Use this information in meetings to help uncover blockages and to identify contributions to the team effort. Seek the assistance of a trained facilitator when the group is having difficulty identifying and removing blockages or when the group is unable to move forward or face its difficulties.

- Continue to refer to the MBTI® results as the group proceeds through the stages of its development.

- Remember that the MBTI® is a tool for self-knowledge and understanding. It helps us to understand behavior but it is not a determinant of behavior. It serves as a guide to understanding behavior but does not explain all behavior.

- See the use of the MBTI® as part of an overall process. Identify and use other tools to help the group become a high-performing team that produces the best possible results.

III. Conclusion

As more work in libraries and information agencies is accomplished by groups of individuals committed to becoming real teams, the recognition of the need for effective team building will increase. The team building process requires individual team members to have a knowledge of their own behavior, an understanding of the range of human behavioral styles, and an appreciation for the variety of differences that exist among people in organizations. A number of individuals who work in libraries and information agencies have had the opportunity to take the MBTI® through personal awareness training, management skills workshops, the 1992 national survey of library and information professionals described in this volume, and in other settings such as church organizations and volunteer organizations. As these individuals spend more of their time working in groups, the MBTI® will become a commonly used tool for team development in our organizations.

NOTES

1. Bruce W. Tuckman and Mary Ann Jensen, "Stages of Small Group Development Revisited," *Group & Organization Studies*, 2 (December 1977): 419-427.

Enhancing Teaching Skills Using the Myers-Briggs Type Indicator

Kathleen Gunning

Introduction

Librarians spend much of their time interacting with other people. They teach people to find information in individual consultations. They make presentations to classes and professional and community groups. As a result, effective teaching skills are essential for library and information professionals. Knowledge derived from the Myers-Briggs Type Indicator (MBTI®) can be used to enhance their skills in making presentations and in teaching others.

The Myers-Briggs Type Indicator provides information on:

(1) where people get their energy (preference for Extraversion or Introversion),
(2) how people gather information about the world (preference for Sensing or Intuition),
(3) how they make decisions based on that information (preference for Thinking or Feeling), and
(4) how much structure or freedom they desire in the outer world (preference for Judging or Perceiving).

Each parameter represents a scale on which a person displays a preference for one of two choices. The findings from these four parameters offer much practical information about the ways that an individual tends to think and behave. There are sixteen possible combinations of the four preferences called types. Persons who share the same type or set of four preferences will exhibit many similar characteristics. Please refer to "Vive la Différence" in this volume for further information about the four scales and sixteen types.

Type and Learning Style

Research using the Myers-Briggs Type Indicator has shown variations in the ways that different types are most comfortable in teaching and learning. For example, knowledge of type offers insight into why a person prefers to learn in situations with more or less structure and more or less class discussion. People tend to perform better in learning environments that are congenial to them, although performance is also influenced by other factors including intelligence, maturity, previous learning experiences, and personal circumstances. Following is a summary of learning style preferences as they relate to the four dimensions measured by the MBTI®.[1]

Extraversion-Introversion
The preference for Extraversion or Introversion relates to the degree to which people benefit from activity while learning and the ways in which people become involved in activity. Extraverts have more need for variety and activity than Introverts and usually like classes to move along rapidly. Learning is facilitated by talking or interacting with others. It may be difficult for them to read for extended periods of time, and they may be able to concentrate more effectively in classes that include group discussion or when they can take periodic active breaks from sedentary tasks such as reading or writing.

The high value that Extraverts place on experience may lead them to begin assignments without much initial planning and proceed on a trial-and-error basis. This approach allows them to think while acting, the method in which they think best. When asked a question, Extraverts tend to begin answering immediately and develop their thoughts as they speak.

Introverts tend to think best when alone or at least uninterrupted, so they need quiet time for study and reflection. They are more comfortable than Extraverts with extended lectures and long periods of reading or writing. Unless they can think about the topics ahead of time, it is more difficult for them to engage in class discussions.

Introverts prefer to think before they act. They often plan extensively, identify possible problems, and develop solutions before beginning an assignment. In responding to a question, Introverts tend to consider their answers before beginning to speak.

Sensing-Intuition
Sensing and Intuitive types concentrate on different aspects of a situation or problem. Sensing types focus on the concrete, specific facts first as a way to begin understanding the situation. They can then build up from the details to a broader grasp of the content or the general theory that explains the specifics.

Given the practical, realistic orientation of Sensors, they prefer learning information that they can use. Clear, concise, and specific instructions are preferred. They tend to enjoy acquiring a skill and improving their performance through repetition. Sensing types would rather complete a task using a technique they have mastered than experiment with new methods.

Intuitive types prefer to begin with an overall theory or general summary of the content to be learned. That context then provides a conceptual framework in which the details can make sense. They enjoy less structured approaches to learning, preferring open-ended assignments that allow them to use their imaginations and explore possibilities. Intuitive types have an aptitude for understanding abstract theories, and their weakness is usually a lack of interest in observing details and learning specific facts or step-by-step procedures.

Thinking-Feeling

The Thinking-Feeling dimension involves the way that people make decisions. In an educational situation, it relates to the factors that motivate people to learn. Thinking types tend to perform best when the performance criteria are clearly articulated. They want to know that their efforts will lead to a greater understanding of the systematic way that the world works. They respond when teachers respect their competence.

In solving problems, Thinking types tend to base their reasoning on rules or principles, and they present their ideas in an orderly, logical manner. Analytical in orientation, they are concerned with weighing the pros and cons, costs and benefits, and impersonally looking at the trade-offs to derive a "best choice" alternative. Thinking types have a higher tolerance than Feeling types for uninteresting tasks if presented with a logical reason. They are likely to focus more on the content of their statements than the process or the effect of their message on other people.

Feeling types want to know that their learning can be used in the service of personally-held beliefs or people they value. Their decision-making process includes clarifying their values, establishing the relative importance of different values, and relating possible outcomes to this hierarchy. For Feeling types, the effects of various alternatives on people must be considered. They are most motivated when their hearts are engaged in their work and may need personal encouragement in order to find a task rewarding. Conflict usually is distasteful to them and inhibits their learning. Their speech is more likely to be expressive and personal, including statements such as "I feel" and "I believe." They may be more concerned with the way that their message is received by the audience than the content of the message itself.

Judging-Perceiving
The Judging-Perceiving dimension is useful in determining whether people prefer structured learning environments. Judging types tend to measure their progress by their accomplishments and function well in learning situations that include goals and deadlines. People with this preference like to have things settled and decided. Closure is important, and they take pleasure in completing assignments.

Perceiving types are less concerned with accomplishing tasks. Their approach to life and work is based on openness, on having options, and on postponing decisions until the moment moves them. They typically view learning situations as flexible and open-ended. Since they prefer spontaneity, highly structured learning situations may lead them to feel restricted and confined. They tend to be risk-takers rather than decision-makers.

Type and Teaching Style
Just as everyone taking a class or hearing a presentation has a type, so does the presenter. Instructors gravitate to the style that is most natural for their type. People tend to teach or make presentations using the same methods that they prefer others to use. This strategy offers some advantages because teaching in their type's style maximizes their strengths and allows them to feel most comfortable in the teaching situation.

However, every audience contains a mixture of types. Any speaker's effectiveness can be increased by awareness of the reasons underlying his or her own preference for certain presentation strategies as well as knowing the strategies most likely to be effective with various segments of the audience. Instructional styles differ as follows:[2]

Extraversion-Introversion
Extraverted instructors are more likely to give people choices about study topics and ways to carry out learning tasks. They are apt to stay attuned to and respond to changes in an individual's attention and activities. Introverted teachers are more attuned to the subject matter they are teaching and to their own thought processes. They often structure learning activities through the specific materials that they choose.

Sensing-Intuition
Sensing instructors are likely to emphasize facts, practical information, and concrete skills. They tend to keep instructional activities centralized and focused on a narrow range of choices. In contrast, Intuitive types focus on concepts and

relationships, and they use facts to understand larger problems. They tend to offer more choices to members of the class.

Thinking-Feeling
Thinking instructors tend to make relatively few comments about the performance of individuals, and these statements are likely to be objective. They tend to have the group spend significant time focused on what the instructor is doing.

Instructors with Feeling preferences are more expressive; they praise and criticize by means of words and body language. They are more likely than Thinking instructors to move among persons and speak to each of them. Students in their classes will be encouraged to spend more time on their own individual work.

Judging-Perceiving
Instructors with a Judging preference are likely to be orderly and adhere to structure and schedules, while those with a Perceiving preference often encourage more movement in the room, more open-ended discussions, and more interaction in study groups.

The following list includes a wide variety of instructional techniques. An instructor could examine the list and identify the teaching or presentation strategies that he or she has used and found effective, those not found to be effective or comfortable, and those never tried. The last section of the list can be used to identify whether concept or activity is the primary instructional focus.[3]

1. Instructional Techniques

___ Brainstorming
___ Case studies
___ Cooperative activities
___ Debate
___ Demonstrations
___ Drill
___ Field trips
___ Games
___ Group discussions
___ Hands-on activities
___ Lecture
___ Note-taking
___ Panels
___ Programmed instruction
___ Projects

___ Readings
___ Role play
___ Spontaneous activities
___ Structured discussions
___ Workbooks
___ Written tests

2. Structure

___ Activity then concept
___ Concept then activity

Following is a suggested set of instructional strategies that are effective for teaching people based on each MBTI® dimension.[4] A consideration of these strategies can also heighten one's awareness of the wide range of available possibilities.

To teach Extraverts:

* Use an interactive presentation style
* Keep procedures uncomplicated
* Emphasize action; keep discussion and events moving
* Focus on the results of the action proposed
* Allow the group to experience learning
* Build in, where possible, group projects and team competitiveness

To teach Introverts:

* Provide written materials ahead of time
* Plan and announce ahead of time the questions to be discussed
* Use a lecture style presentation with overhead transparencies
* Allow for quiet time during the presentation for reflection; do not interrupt when an Introvert is pondering a question
* Avoid making sweeping statements
* Make written assignments as well as oral ones

To teach those with Sensing preferences:

* Present details in an orderly sequence - be precise, step-by-step; include what is to be done, how it is to be done, and why it is to be done this way
* Use demonstrations and pictures to enhance words; allow them to learn by doing
* Be prepared with accurate facts; fill any appendices with supportive data

* Keep answers to questions short and to the point; avoid philosophical or theoretical responses
* Engage as many of the five senses as possible in your presentation/interaction; multimedia presentations are usually effective
* Be careful when recommending a change in the current situation or learning new skills; emphasize the aspects of the situation or the steps in a procedure that will remain the same
* Demonstrate the ways in which skills they already know will aid in learning new skills
* Define goals clearly; draw conclusions that are practical and realistic; make specific and detailed recommendations
* Maintain a results orientation; focus on immediate benefits

To teach those with Intuitive preferences:

* Always include an overview of the content; present overview or summary first; use photos, drawings or charts to help clarify the big picture quickly
* Avoid too much detail
* Focus on the meanings, relationships, and possibilities of the data rather than on the actual data itself
* Discuss philosophical and theoretical principles
* Use confidence and enthusiasm
* Stress long-term planning; indicate challenges and future benefits
* Emphasize new ways of solving problems that can be characterized as innovative, creative, and original

To teach those with Thinking preferences:

* Present the overall logic and state the principles involved
* Use an orderly, chronological presentation style; move from point to point in a logical fashion
* Stress competent handling of issues, achievement motivation, and mastery of tasks
* Identify pros and cons of different options and apply pre-defined criteria that are logical and to the point
* Have and use specific facts and avoid ambiguity
* If there is confusion or disagreement, ask for their help in analyzing the situation
* Use process charts to demonstrate astute planning
* Emphasize fair, impersonal, and impartial treatment of self, others, facts and logic; focus on justice and fairness

To teach those with Feeling preferences:

* Focus on the aspects of the content that relate to human issues
* Use a personable, friendly, less formal style; spend some time in small talk, getting to know each other and getting comfortable
* Use tact, diplomacy, courtesy and a sincere concern for others as the basis of successful interactions
* Show the helpfulness of techniques or ideas to people; focus on the positive aspects of the situation
* Identify others who support these ideas or use these techniques
* Indicate that this is the "right" thing to do
* Emphasize the value of their participation and support

To teach those with Judging preferences:

* Provide well-planned and organized sessions
* Make clear, concise and definite recommendations
* Set standards against which performance will be measured
* Include schedules for activities
* Come to closure on important milestones in the instruction as they occur; tidy up loose ends
* Discuss only the essentials needed for them to make a decision before beginning work
* When unsure of a course of action, use and discuss contingency plans; avoid surprises

To teach those with Perceiving preferences:

* Structure the instruction so that the decisions are made for them; for example, decide which group they will work with and which role they will play
* Provide multiple option pathways with pre-determined selection criteria
* Research thoroughly and have extensive data to support the direction recommended
* Include them in the experiential aspects of class projects
* To establish rapport, attempt to find some common thread in types of shared experiences
* Set up feedback so that they continually receive information that will help them understand things, not manage them

Information about effective learning situations for each of the four dimensions can be combined to produce more detailed descriptions of effective learning strategies for each of the 16 types.[5] A speaker can use the knowledge of his or her own type and the strategies most effective for other types to creatively plan lessons. For example, if the speaker is an Intuitive type, he or she will tend to focus on the "big picture". The most natural sequence for this presenter would be, first, a discussion of a theory or an overall summary of the context and meaning of the topic. Specific facts would then be presented and placed within the broader framework. For an Intuitive, the details of most actual events will be of less interest than the theory or world view or possibilities that the events illustrate.

For the Sensing types in the class, this presentation sequence will probably seem backwards. Without adequate factual preparation, the theory or summary presented may seem to have no basis in reality. The Intuitive speaker who is aware of this difference can occasionally try starting with facts before presenting the summary. The sequence will probably seem awkward and wrong to this speaker when it is first attempted. Consulting a Sensing type in regard to the sequence may be helpful for the Intuitive speaker who is experimenting with Sensing-oriented presentation techniques.

This type of awareness and flexibility can be developed for each dimension of an instructor's MBTI® type. An instructor can experiment with the techniques most effective with students of a different preference and incorporate some into actual classes. Since different types can prefer diametrically opposed instructional methods, it is obviously impossible to employ all of them simultaneously. Depending on the instructor's own type preferences, it may be difficult to experiment with some techniques. For example, an Introverted instructor may find it difficult to encourage and facilitate extensive class discussions.

However, all instructors can understand the legitimacy of different students' preferences and gradually broaden the range of techniques used. It would be advisable to begin this experimentation with methods close to those the instructor prefers. Over time, an instructor can master a set of instructional techniques that offer some accommodation for every type preference.

These techniques can also be used in situations when someone did not understand material the first time it was presented. In addition to reviewing the content, the instructor can consider whether the instructional strategy was a good match for that person. If the instructional technique might be contributing to the comprehension problem, alternative strategies can be employed.

Following is a list of the most and least favored instructional techniques for four MBTI® combinations.[6] Each grouping consists of a two-dimension combination of type preferences. Each of these preference combinations is found in four

MBTI® types, so collectively the set of four includes all sixteen types. These four groupings have theoretical importance that has been widely discussed in other publications.[7] They are frequently used in the literature on the MBTI® to present important differences among types in summary form.

TYPE	FAVORED	LEAST FAVORED
Intuition+Thinking (NT)	Lecture Projects Brainstorming Debate Tests Projects Concept then activity	Repetition Activity then concept
Intuition+Feeling (NF)	Personal focus Small group discussions Cooperative activities Role play Interactive activities Concept then activity	Workbooks Repetition Drill Competitive activities Activity then concept
Sensing+Judging (SJ)	Note-taking Workbooks Hands-on activities Drill Demonstrations Activity then concept	Role play Spontaneous activities Concept then activity
Sensing+Perceiving (SP)	Hands-on activities Projects Games Role play Spontaneous activities Activity then concept	Written tests Workbooks Concept then activity

Distribution of Types

Another consideration in preparing presentations is the rate at which the various MBTI® types occur in the population as a whole. Some types are more prevalent in the general population than others. For example, in the U.S. population, the following approximate distribution has been found:[8]

Extraversion (E)	65%		Introversion (I)	35%	
Sensing (S)	68%		Intuition (N)	32%	
Thinking (T)	61%	men	Feeling (F)	39%	men
	32%	women		68%	women
Judging (J)	55%		Perceiving (P)	45%	

So, for example, a general audience will very likely include many Extraverts and Sensors. Mostly male audiences usually have a high percentage of Thinkers; mostly female audiences usually include a majority of Feelers.

The research reported earlier in this volume shows that certain MBTI® types are represented in greater proportions in the library profession than in the general population.[9] Every profession has its own set of over-represented and under-represented types. As a cautionary note, it is important to mention that every occupation probably includes persons of all MBTI® types, and a person of any MBTI® type could be successful in any occupation. The significant factors are:

(1) the types of skills commonly required in a given occupation will tend to attract some MBTI® types more than others, and
(2) these differences are not accounted for by the variations in the occurrence of MBTI® types in the overall population.

For example, the following four combinations of Sensing-Intuition and Thinking-Feeling preferences are represented in the occupations listed below in higher proportions than in the overall population.[10]

Type	**Occupations**
Intuition+Thinking (NT)	Physical Science Forecasts & Analysis Research Management
Intuition+Feeling (NF)	Behavioral Science Research Literature & Art Teaching
Sensing+Thinking (ST)	Applied Science Business Production Construction

Sensing+Feeling (SF)	Patient Care Community Service Sales Teaching

Detailed information regarding the occurrence of type in specific occupations is available.[11] A librarian can apply information on probable type distribution when preparing a presentation to an occupational group or to students majoring in a specific subject.

It may be helpful to look at the types that occur most frequently among librarians themselves. The preferences found most often in the library profession are Introversion, Intuition, Thinking, and Judging. The research study commissioned by the Association for College and Research Libraries revealed that librarians were represented in greater percentages than the general population in the following nine types:[12]

(1) the four Introverted Intuitive types (INTJ, INFJ, INTP, INFP),
(2) three of four Extraverted Intuitive types (ENTJ, ENFJ, ENTP), and
(3) both Introverted Sensing Judging types (ISTJ, ISFJ).

Librarians were represented in smaller percentages than the general population in the following seven types:

(1) the four Extraverted Sensing types (ESTJ, ESFJ, ESTP, ESFP),
(2) both Introverted Sensing Perceiving types (ISTP, ISFP), and
(3) Extraverted Intuitive Feeling Perceivers (ENFP).

These findings have several implications for librarians as instructors. Extraversion and Sensing are each individually preferred by the majority of the general population. Perceiving is preferred by approximately half the population. Both Extraverted Sensing and Sensing Perceiving types are under-represented in the library profession. These ES and SP types must be taken into account when designing classes or public presentations. Their preferred learning styles will be quite different from those of many librarians.

Another variation from the overall population is the high percentage of librarians, a mostly-female profession, in five of the eight Thinking types. Since the majority of women in the general population have Feeling preferences, female instructors with Thinking preferences may need to cope with students' expectations that their decision-making processes and behavior should be more stereotypically "feminine". The reverse situation can arise for male instructors with Feeling preferences. An understanding of the reasons underlying this potential conflict can help female Thinking instructors and male Feeling instructors develop strategies to cope with this situation.

Staff Training

Another important use of MBTI® information is in staff training. Similar to other instructors, supervisors and staff trainers often assume that members of their staff learn the same way that they do. In libraries, the relatively high percentages of Introverts, Intuitives and Thinkers among librarians may need to teach largely female support staffs who are likely to include greater percentages of Sensing and Feeling types.[13] Awareness of these differences and the design of training programs that address them can lead to more effective and satisfying results.

Conclusion

Knowledge gained from the Myers-Briggs Type Indicator offers librarians a rich array of insights and techniques to enhance teaching skills and design improved staff training programs. These many benefits are well worth the effort to understand and apply this extremely versatile instrument.

REFERENCES AND NOTES

1. George H. Jensen, "Learning Styles" in *Applications of the Myers-Briggs Indicator in Higher Education*, ed. Judith A. Provost and Scott Anchors (Palo Alto, CA: Consulting Psychologists Press, 1987), 183-189.
2. David Keirsey and Marilyn Bates, *Please Understand Me: Character & Temperament Types* (Del Mar, CA: Prometheus Nemesis Book Company, 1984), 155-166.
3. Robert De Groot, *Personality Driven Learning Styles; Designing Training Based on Learning Styles* (Houston, TX: Sales Training America, 1991), 4.
4. Ibid., 9-16.
5. For discussions of individual types, see Alan Brownsword, *It Takes All Types* (Fairfax, VA: Baytree Publishing Co., 1987), 30-84; Keirsey and Bates, *Please Understand*, 167-207; Isabel Briggs Myers and Peter Myers, *Gifts Differing* (Palo Alto: Consulting Psychologists Press, 1980), 85-116; Sandra Hirsh and Jean Kummerow, *LIFETypes* (New York: Warner Books, 1989), 71-270.
6. De Groot, *Personality*, 5.
7. Keirsey and Bates, *Please Understand*, 27-66.

8. Isabel Briggs Myers and Mary H. McCaulley, *Manual: A Guide to the Development and Use of the Myers-Briggs Type Indicator* (Palo Alto: Consulting Psychologists Press, 1985).
9. Mary Jane Scherdin, "Vive la Différence" in this volume, 132.
10. De Groot *Personality*, 8.
11. Myers and McCaulley, *Manual*; Gerald P. Macdaid, *Atlas of Type Tables* (Gainesville, FL: Center for Applications of Psychological Type, 1986); Allen L. Hammer and Gerald P. Macdaid, *MBTI® Career Report Manual* (Palo Alto, CA: Consulting Psychologists Press, 1992).
12. Scherdin, "Vive." 133.
13. Ibid., 148. Nancy Boykin Bounds, Jennifer Patterson, and David T. Bailey, "Working Together" in this volume, 163-166.

Additional Bibliography

Barr, Lee and Norma Barr. *The Leadership Equation.* Austin: Eakin Press, 1989.

Carskadon, Thomas G. "Evaluation of A Self-Paced Introductory Psychology Course as a Function of Psychological Type." *Research in Psychological Type* 3 (1981): 86-88.

Cohen, Stanley R. "Using the MBTI® With Teachers, Supervisors, Administrators and Students: A Program Review." *Research in Psychological Type* 3 (1981): 42-47.

DeNovellis, Richard and Gordon Lawrence. "Correlations of Teacher Personality Variables (Myers-Briggs) and Classroom Observation Data." *Research in Psychological Type* 6 (1983): 37-46.

Hirsh, Sandra Krebs and Jean M. Kummerow. *Introduction to Type in Organizations.* 2nd ed. Palo Alto: Consulting Psychologists Press, 1987.

Hirsh, Sandra Krebs. *Using the Myers-Briggs Type Indicator in Organizations.* Palo Alto: Consulting Psychologists Press, 1985.

Hoffman, Jeffrey L. and Marianne Betkouski. "A Summary of Myers-Briggs Types Indicator Research Applications in Education." *Research in Psychological Type* 3 (1981): 3-41.

Kroeger, Otto with Janet M. Thuesen. *Type Talk at Work.* New York: Tilden Press, 1992.

Kroeger, Otto and Janet M. Thuesen. *Type Talk: Or How to Determine your Personality Type and Change Your Life.* New York: Delacorte Press, 1988.

Lawrence, Gordon. "A Synthesis of Learning Style Research Involving the MBTI®." *Journal of Psychological Type* 8 (1984): 2-15.

Myers, Isabel Briggs. *Introduction to Type.* Palo Alto: Consulting Psychologists Press, 1992.

Provost, Judith A. "`Type Watching' and College Attrition." *Journal of Psychological Type* 9 (1985): 16-23.

Thorne, Avril and Harrison Gough. *Portraits of Type: An MBTI Research Compendium.* Palo Alto: Consulting Psychologists Press, 1991.

Section IV

Looking Ahead

Recruitment Implications, Issues, and Future Action

Margaret Myers

Introduction

The goal of vocational interest inventories and measurement tools is to help people identify careers in which they will be satisfied. Interest inventory tools are used by a variety of age levels, including high school and college students, re-entry persons, employees and others who may be interested in changing careers and are trying to answer the question, "What am I best suited for?"

Target groups for specific interest tools may vary. For example, the authors of the *Manual for the Strong Interest Inventory* have written that "historically, the major use of the Strong has been with adults and l6-, 17-, and l8-year olds. At 17 or l8, interests begin to solidify for most students, and the results begin to be useful for career-planning purposes. By age 21, interests have become even more established, and by 25, interest patterns have stabilized for nearly everyone." [1] However, a career counselor, in reviewing the inventory, suggested that the Strong is best used after age 21 with persons who have had a variety of life experiences, e.g., a job or two, or who have traveled a bit, and who have at least graduated from high school.[2]

The statement from the Strong manual about when interest patterns are established may be of interest to readers of this volume because many librarians come into the profession later in life, sometimes as a second career, after they have raised a family or after working for a number of years as a library support staff member. A 1988 comprehensive study of graduate library and information studies students, their demographics and occupational interests reported that the median age of master's degree students was 35 and that a typical library and information studies student is a part-time, white, geographically place-bound female in her mid-thirties with an undergraduate English or education degree.[3]

How are prospective students attracted to librarianship, and why at a later age when others have identified career interests at an earlier age? Many are attracted to librarianship because of having worked in a library as a support staff person, or student worker, or through knowing a librarian. The *Occupational Entry* study mentioned above found that the highest ranking influence for individuals to pursue a career in librarianship was that of knowing a librarian (35 percent). The influence of family and friends accounted for another 25 percent (some of these may also be librarians but the study did not verify this). Faculty influence accounted for 11 percent of those studied and "objective" influences, such as brochures, articles, counselors, reference books, etc., were only 10 percent. Career interest inventories were not included in the survey questionnaire. Over half (53 percent) of the respondents had worked in a library prior to enrollment in an MLS program.

Little is known about the extent to which vocational interest inventories are responsible for helping individuals choose librarianship as a career, but based on the above survey, they are not a likely influence. It is hoped the research outlined in this volume will increase the likelihood of attracting prospective students through this means, in particular young persons and those who have not had as much contact with libraries and librarians. A number of librarians who are interested in recruitment to the profession have discussed the need to make young people more aware of librarianship as a career.

Recruitment Efforts in Librarianship

Recruitment efforts to interest individuals in a career as a librarian have been undertaken by a variety of groups, such as national and state library associations, state library agencies, library and information studies programs, library systems, and other organizations as well as individuals. Approaches have included distribution of specialized brochures and ads, posters, bookmarks, videos, attendance at career days, mailings to career and guidance counselors or exhibits at their meetings, and recruitment trips to undergraduate campuses, e.g., to historically black colleges and universities. A variety of general career guidance books briefly describe librarianship careers (e.g., the *Occupational Outlook Handbook*). Scholarships have been established by many groups and are a traditional means of attracting prospective students.

Specialized mentoring programs have also been undertaken. For example, a University of California, San Diego librarian has developed an Undergraduate Student Internship Program to introduce student workers who are people of color to various aspects of library work and to encourage them to attend graduate school in library and information studies.[4] Another mentoring program involves partnerships between practitioners in the Los Angeles chapters of REFORMA (the National Association to Promote Library Services to the Spanish-Speaking) and the Black Caucus of the University of California, Los Angeles Graduate School of Library and Information Science to provide one-to-one personal guidance of prospective recruits.[5] A summer intern program in metropolitan Chicago public libraries for college juniors and seniors, funded through the Library Services and Construction Act, introduced individuals who had not worked in libraries previously to career opportunities.[6]

An "Each One Reach One" network established by the American Library Association Office for Library Personnel Resources was built around the premise that individuals come into the field because of knowing a librarian. Each librarian can be involved in identifying potential recruits, mentoring, and helping to provide relevant information that can help someone make a career decision. Although individual recruitment campaigns have sometimes attempted to evaluate results (e.g., how many individuals who were contacted actually went on to get a library science degree?), little overall evaluation as to the effectiveness of the various methods has been undertaken.

Recruitment Issues

The image of librarians often has been cited as a difficulty in recruitment for the profession; yet all professions and occupations have struggled with their image in some way. Efforts in the library profession to promote and expand the public awareness of the library and librarian's role, such as the American Library Association campaigns during National Library Week, should help raise the visibility of librarianship as a career. The lack of understanding of what librarians do has probably hindered recruitment efforts. What we do intellectually isn't always easy to display graphically or describe in written recruitment materials. Increased visibility of the profession and the role of librarians need to be addressed on many levels, from the national to the local. Although organizational efforts are important, the individual librarian as a role model in providing outstanding service to users is perhaps the most powerful recruitment tool.

The lack of an undergraduate major also results in college students not considering library science as a possible track in college or career. In annual polls taken of freshmen by the *Chronicle of Higher Education*, librarianship is not mentioned by new college students as a potential career. Although a few undergraduate library science majors and minors exist (primarily in schools of education), the first professional degree is considered to be at the master's level. Most library and information studies programs prefer a broad undergraduate background in liberal arts and sciences rather than specialization in library science at an undergraduate level. In fact, most any undergraduate major is acceptable for admission into graduate school. (At one time, one of the library and information studies programs advertised on the cover of its school catalog, "What else can you do with a B.A.?") As a librarian, one can use expertise in various subjects to good advantage. The lack of an undergraduate major also results, however, in lack of visibility as a career, especially to younger people who are establishing career interests, as pointed out in the Strong manual.[7]

In addition to the lack of visibility as an undergraduate level discipline, the interdisciplinary nature of the field can be both a strength and a barrier. Drawing on varied disciplines makes it possible to use the many different skills and knowledges that recruits bring to the field. A multitude of different job requirements calls for a whole array of interests and abilities; however, this makes it more difficult to portray the field, particularly in vocational interest inventories, where occupations and professions are often slotted in only one type or category. The scores on the MBTI® and the Strong, as reported elsewhere in this volume, show the many differences between librarians working in the various specializations within librarianship. How will it be possible to interest the variety of persons that can be utilized effectively if profiles of the profession cannot be easily identified?

As a result of the current research outlined in this book, we find that librarians who have been in the profession five years oir less scored higher on the Investigative category of the Strong Interest Inventory. This aspect should be publicized in any new recruitment materials. This could expand the chance that other types of individuals will identify librarianship as a potential career. In addition, the new research on the MBTI® and librarians shows that the field attracts thorough, systematic, consistent, hard-working persons who are careful with procedures and work well in an organized environment as well as those who tend to see the "big picture," need an opportunity to think, plan and create and are attracted to management and leadership positions. Both types are needed in the profession and we need to convey this in recruitment efforts and materials.

Another barrier to recruiting for the profession that is often cited includes low compensation. While salaries are improving in many jurisdictions, particularly for administrators, it may be fruitful to counteract the lack of high salaries by emphasizing the major reasons for engaging in librarianship that are cited by the participants in the current research. Using one's best talents, liking to perform the activities required, and making an important contribution are all given as major attractions.

The lack of mobility of many prospective students coupled with the lack of access to library and information studies programs in some parts of the country is often seen as a further barrier to recruitment. The *Occupational Entry* study cited earlier found that less than 20 percent of the students moved to another state for their library and information studies program, and only about one-third appeared to have mobility after the MLS degree to take a first professional job. In the annual "Placements and Salaries" article in *Library Journal*, 73 percent of the 1992 graduates stayed in the same state in which they earned their MLS.[8] Undoubtedly, the older average age of MLS students accounts for some lack of mobility when individuals have established homes and families. If younger persons are attracted to the field directly from undergraduate programs, difficulties with mobility might be less of a factor.

Many of the library and information studies programs are expanding access to their courses through various distance education methods. In 1991-92, the *Library and Information Science Education Statistical Report* indicated 41 (71 percent) of the ALA accredited master's programs offered one or more courses away from the home campus.[9] Some are given through traditional extension courses that bring faculty to other sites, while others use interactive video and satellite transmissions. To date, most programs still require some residency time on the main campus for completion of a degree. Nevertheless, the capability of reaching beyond the traditional campus will probably increase in the future and make library and information studies more accessible to a wider range of individuals.

Recruitment for the Future

A number of groups and individuals within the library profession have been exploring the human resource needs as well as the knowledge, skills and abilities needed for the changing information environment. Although the economy has hampered most professions and occupations, there are long term needs as retirements take place and information needs grow. A profession-wide consensus has not been reached on what mix of knowledge, skills and abilities are needed in the future. Strong interpersonal and communication skills, ease with technology, and problem-solving ability are often cited as desirable. The need to recruit the "best and the brightest" continues.

At the 1992 American Library Association conference, the Recruitment Assembly participants outlined desirable qualifications for recruits to the profession. These included:

- Service orientation
- Communication skills (oral, written, interpersonal)
- Leadership skills
- Risk-taker
- Curious
- Ability to deal with people of diverse backgrounds
- Entrepreneurs
- Pro-active

- Enthusiasm
- Commitment
- Creative
- Analytical
- Open-minded
- Humanist
- Passionate
- Ethical
- Foreign language knowledge
- Listener
- Detailed oriented
- Flexibility
- Technically competent
- Broad thinker/systems thinking
- Shows initiative
- Bright
- Readers
- Articulate
- Academically gifted
- Specific skill knowledge in subject areas
- Technologically oriented
- Marketing orientation
- Assertive
- Problem solvers
- Caring
- Self-confident

Although it was acknowledged that some of the skills listed above could be taught in library and information studies programs, many are attributes that should already be evident in prospective students. Additionally the Assembly identified priority target groups for recruitment efforts, namely, young persons, support staff, people of diverse racial and cultural backgrounds, and those who are differently abled.

The need for a multicultural workforce to serve in the multicultural society of the future has often been cited in the library literature. The *Occupational Entry* study showed that students with ethnic backgrounds from the traditionally under-represented racial/ethnic groups (i.e., African Americans, American Indian/Alaskan Native, Asian-American, Hispanic) were more apt to be attracted by the opportunities for high tech application and management than Caucasian students. Where will these interests appear in the inventories? Currently, only about 10 percent of MLS students and librarians in the field are people of color.

Suggestions for Future Research and Action

The ACRL Vocational Interest Inventories Task Force continues to monitor librarian profiles on vocational interest inventories. It is often difficult to know where librarianship will be mentioned as a career because of the large number of career publications and inventories, but this is a monitoring task that might be divided among a number of librarians. The staffs of national associations are often asked to comment on drafts of career information; these requests should be more systematically monitored to see if suggested changes are made. The work done by Sheila Delacroix to update the SIGI+ and DISCOVER inventories by consulting a variety of librarians should be used in other publications as well, especially the consensus language developed to update the descriptions of duties and qualifications of librarians.[10]

Discussion should take place among interested professionals on how to measure the effects of the changes in the librarian profiles on the SIGI+, DISCOVER, Strong and MBTI.® Since we do not know how many librarians have used these inventories to define an interest in librarianship, no baseline data exists. Conducting surveys of all incoming MLS students as to how they became interested in library science as a career might prove to have interesting results if carried out by most schools over a period of time. Certainly any follow-up surveys similar to *Occupational Entry* should include career interest inventories as a choice when questioning what influenced a student's selection.

In addition, the inventories might be effectively used once individuals are in graduate school, since initial career choice is followed by choice of a specialty within the field (although in some cases, the specialty might have been the aspect that attracted a person originally). Because of the number of variations in scores on both the Strong and MBTI® by type of library and specialization, the inventories could be used to help new graduates choose specialties that would meet the interests of individuals and lead to the likelihood of greater job satisfaction. Even if the instruments are not administered to individual students, the results of the current research could be disseminated to students and discussed as a part of career exploration sessions during the MLS program. The information can help direct future librarians to a good job "match" where they can take advantage of their preferences and be happy in their work.

The results of the research into the Strong and MBTI® should be examined further by recruiters to help determine what strategies might attract certain types of persons with skills and interests desired by the profession. The groups that are exploring knowledge, skills and abilities desired for the future would also benefit from examining this data. Researchers interested in job satisfaction studies may find useful background information.

Additional attempts by library professionals to have dialogues with career counselors should be made to help counselors understand more fully the diversity of job requirements, skills and knowledge needed to perform successfully in the field as well as the changing and growing environment in which information skills are useful. As pointed out in this volume, a diversity of interests and personality types exist among librarians. This information needs to be conveyed to career and guidance counselors who may be operating from an outmoded stereotype of the profession.

Future efforts to recruit the "best and the brightest" to the profession can emphasize the wide variety of settings and functions in which the library and information profession is practiced as well as the diversity of interests, skills, knowledge and personality types that are needed within the profession.

REFERENCES AND NOTES

1. Jo-Ida Hansen and David P. Campbell, *Manual for the Strong Interest Inventory*, 4th ed. (Palo Alto, CA: Consulting Psychologists Press, 1985), 17.
2. "Strong Interest Inventory," *Career Planning and Adult Development Journal* 7 (Spring 1991): 29-31.
3. Kathleen M. Heim and William E. Moen, *Occupational Entry: Library and Information Science Students' Attitudes, Demographics and Aspirations Survey* (Chicago: American Library Association Office for Library Personnel Resources, 1989).
4. Tami Echavarria, "More Minority Librarians: A Recipe for Success." *Library Personnel News* 5 (January-February 1991): 2, 4.
5. "California Program Recruits Latino Librarians," *Library Personnel News* 5 (January-February 1991): 3.
6. Miriam Pollack et al., *Recruiting for the Library Profession: A Mentoring/ Intern Process* (Chicago: American Library Association Office for Library Personnel Resources, 1992).
7. Hansen and Campbell, *Manual*, 17.
8. Fay Zipkowitz, "Placements and Salaries 1992: Few Graduates but Salaries Climb." *Library Journal* (October 15, 1993): 30-36.
9. Association for Library and Information Science Education, *Library and Information Science Education Statistical Report* (Raleigh, N.C.: ALISE, 1993), 252-256.
10. Sheila Ann Delacroix, "SIGI PLUS: A Case Study in Changing Images" in this volume.

Finale: Reflections, Conclusions, Questions . . .

Sandra Pfahler

Introduction

The author came into this project with a somewhat skeptical and cynical outlook about the value of personality, interest, and skill inventories. Her belief was that learning more about individuals to gain a better understanding of groups would not have a practical use. She also thought that additional considerations, such as gender, family influence, and ethnicity play a significant role in career decision-making. She was concerned that the information collected from the various surveys reported in this book would be too imprecise to initiate any significant change in the profession of librarianship. She doubted that librarians could have any real influence on the public's perception of them.

Reviewing the data found in the various studies reported in this book modified her opinions. A reasonably clear profile of the librarian of today emerges. Ideas on how to use the information to create positive change in the field are presented.

Changing the Image

One of the reasons for publishing the research on librarians' profiles from vocational inventories is stated in the preface of this book. The stereotype of the librarian is a negative one in the minds of many people. However, before librarians can be successful in changing their public image, they must have a clear understanding of who they are. The review of the literature and the studies reported in this book on the Myers-Briggs Type Indicator (MBTI®), Campbell Interest and Skill Survey, ACT Interest Inventory, and Strong Interest Inventory provide a great deal of information on the interests, skills, and personalities of librarians.

In addition, information about librarians gained through these studies has practical applications as people go about their daily responsibilities as librarians. The chapters covering team building, teaching, and learning styles offer effective ideas for using the MBTI®in the workplace.

Another reason for publishing the data is to improve the recruitment of people who can strengthen the role of libraries and librarians in society. The chapter on recruitment implications by Margaret Myers describes current efforts and gives suggestions based on knowledge gained from the studies reported here.

Changing the image of librarians and recruiting the appropriate people into the profession are not simple tasks. The story told by Sheila Ann Delacroix of the energy that went into making changes in the SIGI PLUS career guidance tool is an example of the struggle ahead. Educators responsible for recruiting and instructing new librarians need to take the lead in providing the most current and comprehensive profile of the profession. Career counselors and developers of self-directed career guidance tools must be given a clear understanding of the roles and responsibilities of librarians. They cannot base their work on the negative image of librarians spending the day chasing naughty children around the library.

Assistance is found by examining the favorable and positive information shown in these studies in order to gain a better understanding of the profiles of the profession. Such understanding can further the goal of building a stronger and more influential profession by publicizing what has been learned and promoting the role of librarians in society.

Deborah Grimes' review of the literature found positive characteristics in most past studies. Librarians are described as well-adjusted, orderly, conscientious, responsible, self-sufficient, intelligent, achievement-oriented, kind, imaginative and helpful. These descriptive words portray a strong and favorable image of librarians.

Early studies also reveal some negative characteristics found in librarians. They are described as submissive in social situations, aloof, insecure, over-controlled, suspicious, apprehensive, tense, and lacking in self-confidence, decision-making skills, leadership qualities, vigor, and ambition.

Naturally, labeling certain factors as negative is, to a certain extent, determined by an individual's values. Perhaps a better approach is to say that the profession may have too many people of similar type or not enough variety of types. There is a need for diversity. The unfavorable information gives a clear picture of where changes must occur if the public image is to improve and the number of talented and creative people attracted to the profession is to increase. Can the profession build on the strengths revealed by the positive characteristics of librarians in these early studies? How strongly do the negative characteristics of the past influence the public image of librarians today?

ACT Interest Inventory

The ACT Interest Inventory survey, conducted and reported by Mary Jane Scherdin, places librarians in Region 9 but very near two job families in Region 10 on the ACT World-of-Work Map. The two job families are the Applied Arts (Visual) Family in the Arts Job Cluster and the Social Sciences Family in the Science Job Cluster. Membership in the Applied Arts Family integrates librarians with floral designers, merchandise displayers, commercial artists, fashion designers, photographers, interior designers, architects, and landscape architects.

Are librarians' talents best used to maintain bulletin boards, mount exhibits, and organize work space? If not, a close look at the Applied Arts Family should reveal some useful information. Certainly creativity, a characteristic of the Artistic type, can be used to design and market services. The fact that the library profession offers the opportunity to look at old methods of doing things in new and imaginative ways is something to be promoted.

Membership in the Social Sciences Family relates librarians to marketing research analysts, anthropologists, economists, political scientists, psychologists, and sociologists. Obviously, the librarian as researcher and scholar is most comfortable in this family. Researchers have the opportunity to identify problems and solve them by drawing conclusions based on the collection and analysis of data. Librarians responsible for reference activities help their patrons solve problems using these same skills. A public image of the librarian as problem-solver would be quite an improvement over what exists in the minds of many people today.

Region 9, the home of librarians, falls between the Science and the Creative Arts models, also described as the Investigative and Artistic models. Placement between science and the humanities seems appropriate for librarians because of the balance it offers, yet few science majors become librarians. Can the ACT data, which finds librarians interested in research and investigation, be used to recruit people with a background in science? This idea warrants some study.

Investigative is defined as investigating and attempting to understand, through reading, research, and discussion, phenomena in the natural sciences. Artistic is defined as expressing oneself through activities such as painting, designing, singing, dancing, and writing as well as artistic appreciation of such activities (e.g., listening to music, reading literature.) Both models emphasize reading.

Perhaps the librarians who entered the profession mainly because they love to read made a wise choice after all. Can the relationship described here between the sciences and humanities be used to promote librarianship and market services? Does the profession take too lightly the need to recruit people who know the joy of reading?

The World-of-Work Map also includes a Social Service model, which covers Regions 1 and 12, and sits quite a distance from Region 9. The Social Service model is defined as helping, enlightening, or serving others through activities such as teaching and counseling, working in service-oriented organizations, and engaging in social/political studies. These activities seem to be a good fit for librarians in public service and instruction. However, few respondents placed in this area of the map. Why is that? Is another study using the ACT needed for librarians? Scherdin's study examined the differences and similarities between librarians and information specialists. She states in the report on her ACT study that work tasks need to be analyzed in order to make a decision on the appropriate job family. The MBTI®/Strong study collected data on tasks performed by participants that allowed a more detailed breakdown relating tasks to interests. Perhaps a study on the order of Scherdin's work on the MBTI® and Strong is due for the ACT.

Campbell Interest and Skill Survey

The Campbell Interest and Skill Survey, a recently developed instrument, is described by Richard Johnson and others. Since a limited sample was used, further study with a larger number of participants is needed. However, the results are interesting. The instrument, which measures interests and skills, includes Orientation scales, Occupational scales, and Special scales. The Orientation scales include seven general categories (Influencing, Organizing, Helping, Creating, Analyzing, Producing and Adventuring.)

The survey indicates that librarians score highest in the Creating category and lowest in the Adventuring category. Specific interests and skills of librarians are writing, international activities, art/design, plants/gardens, animal care, science, performing arts, fashion, culinary arts, and farming/forestry.

The interests and skills listed above reflect many of the results of the ACT Interest Inventory survey, especially relating to the Applied Arts Family. Someone who understands both the joy of reading and the joy of cooking will find happiness as a librarian, but is that enough? Librarians reveal a broad spectrum of interests. This information is ideal to use in the recruitment of a variety of types and to improve the image of those already working as librarians.

What is most revealing about librarians in the Campbell survey is that they score relatively low in the Influencing category where most of the management occupations are found. Low interest and a low perceived skill level exists in counseling, leadership, public speaking, supervision and risk/adventure, all characteristics which should be found in effective and successful managers. Occupations that are not of interest to librarians, and for which librarians believe they are not skilled, include hotel manager, CEO/president, and school superintendent.

The Scherdin MBTI® study reported that the two most frequently found types among the library profession are the same types that are found most frequently in managerial positions. However, the interest level, as reported in the Campbell survey, does not indicate that librarians are strongly inclined toward taking positions of leadership.

Library managers almost always come from the ranks. There is a prejudice against hiring managers from outside the profession. Is that wise considering the low interest shown by librarians? More people in the field with skill in leadership and public speaking could have a positive influence on how society views librarians. More risk takers who have the management skills to back them up, could create excitement in a profession that some outsiders view as dull. Can the library field entice people who are interested and skilled in dynamic leadership management?

Often a discussion of the lack of highly skilled library leaders evolves into the lament that librarians are not paid enough to attract this type of person to the profession. This conclusion needs to be examined more closely. It may be that most librarians are underpaid. However, many library managers are well-paid. One negative aspect of the public image of librarians that needs to be dispelled is that all librarians are underpaid. Once that perception is corrected, salaries of all librarians may improve. The profession needs to find new ways of promoting better salaries. Emphasizing the fact that some librarians are paid well and campaigning to improve the public's understanding of the value of librarians should have a positive effect on salaries.

Job Satisfaction

An artistic animal-lover who enjoys cooking and reading and who can demonstrate strong management and leadership skills, including risk-taking, should be able to find a challenging job, a good salary and a niche in librarianship. Will s/he be satisfied in the profession? If not, why not?

Consulting Psychologists Press, the publisher of the Strong Interest Inventory, has certain requirements for eligibility to participate in a sample group of people representing an occupation. One requirement is that participants be satisfied with their work. Mary Jane Scherdin worked with CPP to update the librarian profile in the Strong Interest Inventory. She found that 93% of the ALA and SLA members who responded to her survey stated satisfaction with their work.

More research is needed to uncover additional information on why some librarians are dissatisfied with their chosen profession. Efforts to recruit people who have personalities, skills and interests different from the norm could be improved with this information. The new recruits need to stay to make a difference. Surveying a cross section of all librarians, not only association members, might find a larger sample of dissatisfied librarians.

Strong Interest Inventory

Results of the Strong Interest Inventory show librarians as dominant on the Artistic Theme. The pattern continues, beginning with the placement of librarians in the Applied Arts Family of the ACT Interest Inventory, in the Creating Category of the Campbell Interest and Skill Inventory, and on the Artistic Theme of the Strong Interest Inventory. The definition of the Artistic type includes the words expressive, original, intuitive, creative, nonconforming, introspective and independent. These characteristics do not describe the stereotypical librarian. Using this positive information, librarians need to invest their natural creativity in devising ways of promoting the field using this positive information.

Librarians score lower on the Realistic, Enterprising and Social themes in the Strong Interest Inventory survey. What is the profession missing by having fewer people of these types? Robust, rugged, and practical, Realistic types have the potential for mechanical ability and good motor coordination. These people can be mechanics, engineers, electricians, and tool designers. Librarians have become more dependent on machines. Those with Realistic interests are needed to assist in the design and creation of technology that supports systems and services.

The Enterprising type includes people who like to take financial and interpersonal risks and to participate in competitive activities. They have the potential for verbal skills suited to public speaking, persuading and selling, and they seek positions of leadership, power, and status. Librarianship could use more strong leaders. To get them, the profession needs to be more attractive to the Enterprising type. How is that done? As stated earlier, one way is to improve salaries. Another is to emphasize the role librarians have in fund-raising and development. Understanding the role of librarians as managers of units within larger organizations (e.g., governments, educational institutions, and corporations) should also help Enterprising types realize their leadership talents would be put to good use in libraries.

The Social category includes people who like to help and understand others and who are interested in teaching. Librarians put great value on their public service role; reference and instruction responsibilities are of the highest priority in most libraries. Yet the Social type is lacking in librarianship. What does this mean? Is the quality of reference and instruction work suffering because of it? If so, does this deficiency affect the commitment to public service and consequently the public's perception of librarians? Opportunities need to be identified to promote the reference and instruction responsibilities of librarianship in order to recruit more people with Social interests into the profession.

Myers-Briggs Type Indicator

The Myers-Briggs Type Indicator is one of the most popular tools used in the workplace today. Kathleen Gunning notes that a variety of different types can enhance an organization. Maureen Sullivan explains how the MBTI® is used in team building as a method to help people appreciate the variety of personalities in an organization. Of course, this is assuming there is variety in the organization.

Mary Jane Scherdin's MBTI® survey found some striking similarities among librarians. Sixty-three percent (63%) have the Introversion preference. Sixty-nine percent (69%) of male librarians and 58% of female librarians have the Thinking preference. Fifty-nine percent (59%) are Intuitive types, and 66% percent are Judging types. This may not make for a great deal of variety in a single library, particularly a small one.

The Texas study reported by Nancy Boykin Bounds and others included all staff employed in libraries. The numbers are somewhat more balanced. Fifty-nine percent (59%) are Introverts; 57% are Sensing types; 52% have the Thinking preference; and 63% are Judging types. This is evidence for increasing the involvement of support staff in libraries. They can play a valuable role as members of teams, committees, or self-directed work groups in libraries that are structured around a participatory model.

The greatest number of librarians in the MBTI®study conducted by Scherdin fall into the ISTJ four-letter type. ISTJs are serious, quiet, practical, orderly, matter-of-fact, logical, realistic, and dependable. INTJ is the second most frequently found type. These librarians are skeptical, critical, independent, and determined.

They have creative minds, strong organizational skills, and are relentless innovators. The third most frequently found type, INTP, is most interested in ideas. INTPs are quiet, reserved, logical and analytical. The fourth highest type, and the one found most frequently among librarians who were tested between 1971 and 1984, is ISFJ. An ISFJ is quiet, friendly, responsible, conscientious, thorough, painstaking, accurate, loyal, considerate, and perceptive.

Some of the words used to illustrate the most frequent MBTI® types could be used to describe the stereotypical librarian, at least the one who frowns and shushes. Librarians must identify and accentuate the characteristics listed above that will positively influence people outside the profession and change the image of the past.

Most of the people who enter the library field are different from the general population. Sixty-three per cent (63%) of librarians are Introverts compared to 35% Introverts in the general population. Fifty-nine percent (59%) of librarians are Intuitive compared to 32% of the general population. In a field dominated by women, 58% of female librarians are the Thinking type compared to 32% of women in the general population. Sixty-six per cent (66%) of librarians are Judging compared to 55% of the general population.

Undoubtedly these differences influence the public image of librarians and make recruitment more challenging. Do the differences also influence how librarians view their user population? Librarians who have a good understanding of these differences will make better decisions regarding services and collections, because the decisions will be based on users' needs and perceptions. The more informed librarians are about library users, the better able they are to design and market services and build collections. The fact that librarians' personalities are different from the general population should not be a problem as long as the differences are understood.

Conclusion

The studies reported here contain data valuable to the field of librarianship. This is especially true of the Scherdin survey using the Strong Interest Inventory and the MBTI.® In the preface of this volume, Anne Beaubien expresses concern that the profession is not attracting the versatile, intelligent and creative people society needs as the information specialists of the future. To improve the recruitment function, more information is needed on the skills required of the information specialists of the future. That knowledge will come when the profession has a better understanding of the responsibilities and skills of today's successful librarians.

The Scherdin study included questions regarding responsibilities and job activities. Respondents were asked to indicate how much of their working time was devoted to specific job activities. A close look at this data should shed more light on the responsibilities of the librarian in society today. That data, combined with all that is now known about skills, personalities, and interests, should help create a profile of the librarian of the future.

Specific knowledge, skills, and abilities are needed by all people to meet the demands of the age of information. Society is challenged by rapid and constant change in technology and telecommunication development. The challenge can be met and conquered to a large degree by problem solvers, systems analysts, systems designers, and project managers. Librarians are these people. The various inventories found them to be investigators, researchers, artists, readers, organizers, designers, and analysts.

These are the characteristics the library profession should be extolling to recruit more talented people into the field. They create a powerful image of the librarian that will destroy the stereotype and strengthen the role of librarianship in society.